BAKING FOR THE HOLIDAYS
AND ALL WINTER LONG

From Sarah Kieffer, author of *100 Cookies* and beloved baker behind *The Vanilla Bean Blog*, comes this sweet cookbook on holiday baking at home—the kind of indulgent, shareable, calories-don't-count baking we dream about all year round. In these pages, you'll find recipes for classic and unique treats for holiday brunches, seasonal parties, cookie swaps, and special dinners; edible gifts to give family and friends; and delicious baked goods to get you through the long winter months after the holidays have ended. Belly-warming and delectable, these recipes include:

- *Classic Cinnamon Rolls*
- *Meyer Lemon–White Chocolate Scones*
- *Pear-Almond Danish Braid*
- *Triple Chocolate Peppermint Bark*
- *Hot Chocolate Cake*
- *Crème Brûlée Pumpkin Pie*
- *and More!*

A festive essential, perfect for a cozy day, *Baking for the Holidays* is the frosting on top of a wonderful, scrumptious holiday season, year after year. So, get the butter out of the fridge, grab the sugar, and roll up your sleeves! Let's get baking.

BAKING FOR THE HOLIDAYS

50+ Treats for a Festive Season

BAKING FOR THE HOLIDAYS

CHRONICLE BOOKS
SAN FRANCISCO

Sarah Kieffer

DEDICATION

This book is dedicated to my Mom, Patricia Hesse, who never liked baking but still always baked with us, and who didn't have fond memories of Christmases past but made sure her kids had a bright Christmas present and future. I love you.

And to Maddie and Ellie, here's to many holiday seasons baking with your Auntie. xx

Library of Congress Cataloging-in-Publication Data

Names: Kieffer, Sarah, author.
Title: Baking for the holidays : 50+ treats for a festive season / Sarah Kieffer.
Description: San Francisco : Chronicle Books, [2021]. | Includes bibliographical references and index.
Identifiers: LCCN 2020058057 | ISBN 9781452180755 (hardcover) | ISBN 9781452183466 (ebook)
Subjects: LCSH: Holiday cooking. | Christmas cooking.
Classification: LCC TX772 .K535 2021 | DDC 641.5/68--dc23
LC record available at https://lccn.loc.gov/2020058057

Manufactured in China.

Design by Lizzie Vaughan.
Typesetting by AJ Hansen.
Typeset in Intervogue and Quincy.

Photograph on page 110: Shutterstock, Anton Buymov.

10 9 8 7 6 5 4 3 2 1

Chronicle books and gifts are available at special quantity discounts to corporations, professional associations, literacy programs, and other organizations. For details and discount information, please contact our premiums department at corporatesales@chroniclebooks.com or at 1-800-759-0190.

Chronicle Books LLC
680 Second Street
San Francisco, California 94107
www.chroniclebooks.com

CONTENTS

1

Morning Breads and Pastries

2

Holiday Desserts

3

Gift Giving

4

Beyond Christmas

5

Extras

Introduction

My family had an old, rugged, fake Christmas tree that didn't require water, even though my mom always pined for a real, living tree to place in our front window. To my ten-year-old self, however, there was nothing like the thrill of my dad pulling out the giant, torn box it was kept in from the laundry room. He would mutter under his breath as he assembled it in our tiny family room; it was miserable work and that darned hunk of metal and plastic wasn't well made, but my siblings and I were oblivious to his mumbling, dancing around the half-assembled tree, singing songs full of holly and cheer. *Joy to the world!* My younger sister and I would grab the tree decorations, fighting over who got to hang the prettiest ornaments. My little brother would tackle our legs, knocking baubles and angels out of our hands while singing out of key. The smell of sugar cookies, ornately decorated by all of us just moments before, filled the room. My mom would tend a simmering pot of hot chocolate, complete with tiny marshmallows. It was the day after Thanksgiving, and the countdown to Christmas had officially begun.

Although my mom has never enjoyed baking and cooking as a pastime (she often refers to her kitchen as "the worst room in the house") she actively made baking a part of our holiday season. Cookies in all the classic shapes and sizes were a tradition: snowmen, angels, trees, and stars were cloaked in ungodly amounts of red and green sprinkles. Peanut butter chocolate kiss cookies, Rice Krispies wreaths complete with Red Hots, seven-layer bars, and Russian tea cakes were also on the menu. Mini quick breads and apple pies occasionally showed up on the countertops. There were even a few years my mom dabbled in candy making and spritz cookies; we were fascinated by the special presses and molds she used to make these treats. If my dad wasn't working, he was in charge of music, and Amy Grant's *A Christmas Album* or Evie's *Christmas Memories* could be heard playing in the background while we baked together, along with our cassette tape of *Christmas with the Chipmunks*, to my mom's dismay. My sister and I spent much time fighting over cookie cutters and sprinkles, and my little brother would help the edible decorations find their way to the kitchen floor. When our work was complete, we were immediately sent off to the neighbors to deliver our creations. There would be a brief scuffle outside over who got to hold the most tempting bundle of treats, and one of us would inevitably fall down on the snowy sidewalk leading from the house. Coated in snow, we would pass our goodie plates out to eager, smiling faces who would hastily hand us their own homemade treats in return. We'd usually return home with more cookies than we started with, and after eating our fill, the leftover treats would be moved to the basement freezer, where my sister and I would take turns sneaking downstairs and nibbling on them when no one was watching. *He sees you when you're sleeping! He knows when you're awake!* my parents would remind us when we emerged from the basement with chocolate-coated fingers and faces. We were bordering on the precipice of belief and myth, but no matter the sermon, cookies always won the discourse in our hearts.

Christmas Eve would finally arrive, and we'd pile in the car with trays of cookies on our lap, headed to Grandma's house in the city. Her long, antique dining room table would be carefully covered in her mother's lace, already stacked high with food when we arrived. In one corner, tiny meatballs were bubbling in a slow cooker full of thick sauce, surrounded by bowls full of potato chips in every color. Another corner of the table would host my grandma's stash of roasted salty mixed nuts, along with fragile glass

trays piled with black olives and carrot sticks. Without fail, my sister and I would find cozy spots by the cheese tray to fill our small faces full; we'd alternate between devouring appetizers and homemade cookies while the adults had their backs turned.

Hours later, after much ripping through paper and screaming with excitement at our new toys (the Barbie McDonald's set was a particularly exciting year), we would leave for home, our minds racing with dancing sugarplums, minus the plums. My parents would drive us around the city to look at all the Christmas lights, and we would somehow organically nestle into stillness, singing softly together: *Silent night, Holy night.* Slowly, for a brief moment, our young hearts prepared room.

But Christmas morning set them on fire again, and we bounced off the walls with excitement, running toward that old, plastic tree and the possibilities contained underneath. Most years my dad spent much of November and December working overtime so he could watch his children's faces light up at the sight of toys and goodies, but reading the Christmas story out loud was first on his list of things to do. My dad's long, thin fingers would turn each delicate page of his Bible, and we would tap our pajamaed feet impatiently while we stared at the pile before us. When Luke was finally finished recounting his version of things, we would dive in—paper thoughtlessly torn, the house covered in every kind of wrapping. We would then spend the day, just the five of us, reading new books, playing new games, nibbling on leftover cookies and bars, sipping hot apple cider,

and singing along to the carols on the radio. *Let your heart be light,* they whispered on and off, and we subconsciously nodded along, our troubles out of mind for the sweet, fleeting hours of Christmas Day.

Many holiday seasons have come and gone since then, and while I hold all these child-hood memories dear, my yearly celebration looks much different now. Ella Fitzgerald's soaring alto swings for us instead of the falsetto of the Chipmunks. Our family dinners and present openings are in different rooms in different houses, and my own children are the ones fighting over cookie cutters. The one thing that has remained constant over time is the hours we spend baking; our tradition of spending time together in the kitchen creating cookies and bars and candy for

family and neighbors is an important ritual in the months leading up to the New Year. And while only a few of the recipes have made their way from Christmas past to our current kitchen, still we merrily share them with our family and neighbors; the act of creating and giving is central to our celebration.

While my nostalgia is built around specific Christmas traditions, my hope for all who use this book is that the recipes and notes contained among the pages bring comfort and cheer to your own festivities and families, however they are shaped and chosen. No matter how or when you partake of your traditions, may the universal themes of the season—joy, light, hope, and peace—surround and keep you as you continue to give and receive in your own beautiful ways.

While my family celebrates Christmas, this book is really for the months that come before and after it, for the days that we refer to as "The Holidays" but actually just encompass the glow of enjoying time with those we love at the end of the year. This book is divided into five chapters. First: Morning Breads and Pastries. This is a chapter for lots of yeasted baking for out-of-town guests, brunches, morning coffee dates, get-togethers, and Christmas morning. I included classics like Classic Cinnamon Rolls (page 25) and Powdered Sugar Donuts (page 59), but also some twists on old standards with a Cranberries and Cream Danish (page 47), a Coffee-Cardamom Monkey Bread (page 54), and Panettone Scones (page 67). Chapter 2 is Holiday Desserts, which includes desserts for dinner parties, open houses, Thanksgiving, and of course, Christmas dinner itself. Here you'll find Carrot Cake with Burnt Honey Buttercream

(page 84); Apple, Caramel, and Hard Cider Pie (page 96); and Chocolate Mint Ice Cream Pie (page 103). Chapter 3 looks outward to Gift Giving: little treats for your neighbors, coworkers, family, and friends. Modern Fruit Cakes (page 135) are a personal favorite, as are Peanut Butter Cups (page 121), Florentines (page 138), and Triple Chocolate Peppermint Bark (page 123). Chapter 4 stretches beyond the season into those long, endless, "always winter, never Christmas" January days. Recipes focus on in-season citrus flavors and keeping warm: Blood Orange Turnovers (page 160), Lemon Pull-Apart Bread (page 154), and Hot Chocolate Cake (page 178). And, as always, I have a chapter of Extras, recipes to use with other recipes in this book or as stand-alone treats: No-Churn Ice Cream (page 196), Candied Nuts (page 207), Pastry Cream (page 199), Lemon Curd (page 208), and the like.

A FEW IMPORTANT NOTES ON TECHNIQUE

General Baking Advice

It is vital to read the entire recipe all the way through before beginning a baking project. It is essential to know all the ingredients, details, and timing at the start to help ensure the recipe succeeds. Once you feel confident about how a recipe works, you can then think about personalizing it.

Measuring Flour

Throughout this book, 1 cup of all-purpose flour equals 142 g (or 5 oz). This is on the higher end of the scale (a cup of flour can range anywhere from 4 to 5 oz, depending on the baker), but I found that after weighing many cups of flour and averaging the total, mine always ended up around this number. Because most people do scoop flour differently, I highly encourage the use of a scale when measuring ingredients to get consistent results and have provided weight measurements on page 216. I recommend the dip-and-sweep method for flour if you are not using a scale: Dip the measuring cup into the bag or container of flour, then pull the cup out with the flour overfilling the cup. Sweep the excess off the top with a knife so that you have a level cup of flour.

Measuring Semisolids

Yogurt, sour cream, peanut butter, pumpkin purée, and the like are all examples of semisolids: ingredients that fall somewhere between a liquid and a solid. I always measure these types of ingredients in a liquid measuring cup, which gives a little more volume than a dry measuring cup because the cup is slightly bigger. If you are not using a scale to measure these ingredients, I highly recommend using a liquid measuring cup so your baked goods will turn out correctly.

A Pinch of Salt

A pinch of salt is called for occasionally throughout these pages. It is a little more than ⅛ teaspoon, but less than ¼ teaspoon.

Egg Wash

To make an egg wash, use a fork to whisk 1 large egg, a pinch of salt, and 1 tablespoon of water together in a small bowl.

Lining Cake Pans and Loaf Pans with Parchment Paper

Lining pans with a parchment paper sling results in an easy release. To line a square or rectangular pan, cut two pieces of parchment paper the same width as the bottom of your pan and long enough to come up and over the sides. Spray the pan with cooking spray, then place the pieces of parchment in the pan, perpendicular to each other so each side has a bit of parchment overhang, making sure to push the sheets into the corners.

To line a round pan, cut circles of parchment paper the same size as the bottom of your cake pan. Use a generous amount of room-temperature butter to coat the sides and bottom of the pan with a thin, even layer that covers the entire inside surface. Place the parchment circle in the bottom of the pan. Coat the paper with another thin, even layer of butter (or cooking spray). Place 2 to 3 tablespoons of flour in the cake pan and move the pan around, distributing the flour so it evenly coats the butter. When the butter is coated, gently tap the pan upside down over your sink to remove any excess flour.

Tempering Chocolate

Tempering chocolate allows it to set properly and gives the chocolate a glossy, smooth finish. Throughout the book I use a "cheater's method" to temper chocolate, which is to melt most of the chocolate called for, and then finely chop the remaining few ounces of chocolate and stir it into the melted chocolate until it is also melted, so that the finished, melted chocolate ends up around 88°F [31°C]. This method isn't foolproof, but it's worked for me 99 percent of the time.

INGREDIENTS

The following is a list of ingredients used in this book. Most of these ingredients should be available at your local grocery store, but for the few that are specialty items or hard to find, I have included a resources section at the back of the book (page 218) to help you locate them.

Dairy and Eggs

BUTTER • All the recipes in this book call for unsalted butter. If you are a fan of salted butter and prefer to use it instead, you will want to use a little less salt overall in the recipe. European-style butter cannot always be swapped for regular butter; the high fat content can cause extra spreading or other problems. If European-style butter is used, it will be noted in the recipe. For

grocery store brands, I prefer Land O'Lakes Unsalted Butter. I do not suggest substituting oils for butter.

CREAM CHEESE • I prefer Philadelphia brand cream cheese in my recipes; I find it tastes best overall and gives baked goods a creamier feel.

CRÈME FRAÎCHE • This matured cream has a tangy flavor and a smooth texture. It is used occasionally in this book, and there is a recipe for making it at home in the Extras chapter (page 205). I use Vermont Creamery crème fraîche when purchasing a store-bought brand.

EGGS • All the recipes here call for grade A large eggs. In its shell, a large egg should weigh 2 oz [57 g]. For egg-rich recipes (such as Pastry Cream, page 199) I like to use local, farm-fresh eggs because they typically have beautiful, orange yolks. If the recipe calls for room-temperature eggs, you can place the eggs in a large bowl, cover them with warm water, and let them sit for 10 minutes. If you need to separate the egg whites and the yolk, it's generally easier to start with a cold egg because the yolk will be firmer.

HEAVY CREAM • Look for a heavy cream that is pasteurized, not ultra-pasteurized, if possible, especially when making crème fraîche. Heavy cream is also known as double cream.

MILK • I tested all the recipes in this book with whole milk. I don't recommend replacing most recipes with a lower-fat milk, as this can possibly change the outcome of the recipe.

Cooking Oils

CANOLA OIL • Canola oil is the most common oil you'll find called for in this book because of its neutral flavor, but grapeseed oil is another good neutral option.

OLIVE OIL • Use a good-quality extra-virgin olive oil so the flavor shines in the final product.

TOASTED SESAME OIL • I love the flavor of toasted sesame oil, and while it is usually used in savory cooking, I've found pairing it with sugar is delicious.

Salt and Spices

FLEUR DE SEL • This is a delicate, moist salt that is usually used as a finishing salt. Because the crystals are larger, the salt takes longer to dissolve, and the taste lingers a bit longer.

SPICES • Make sure your spices haven't been sitting in your cupboard for years before using them. Although they appear to last forever, they do have a shelf life and can grow stale or rancid over time. Spices retain their freshness for 6 months to a year.

TABLE SALT • I use table salt rather than kosher salt in all the recipes in this book unless otherwise noted.

Sweeteners

BROWN SUGAR • Light brown sugar was used for recipe testing in this book. Brown sugar contains more acidity and moisture than light brown sugar, and isn't always a good substitute.

CONFECTIONERS' SUGAR • Confectioners' sugar is also known as powdered sugar and icing sugar.

CORN SYRUP • Do not substitute dark corn syrup for light; it has a more robust flavor and is not a good replacement in these recipes.

GRANULATED SUGAR • Granulated sugar (also known as white sugar) was used to test all the recipes in this book. Organic sugar can be substituted, but please note that it often has a coarser grain than regular white sugar, which means it won't melt as quickly as more finely ground sugar. If organic sugar is preferred, it can be processed in a food processor until it is finely ground before using.

SANDING SUGAR • Sanding sugar is a large-crystal sugar that doesn't dissolve while baking. It is used mainly for decorating.

Flour

ALL-PURPOSE FLOUR • All the recipes in this book were tested with Gold Medal unbleached all-purpose flour, unless otherwise noted in the recipe. Different brands of flours have varying levels of protein, which can result in very different outcomes when baking. I've found Gold Medal to be the best option for the recipes in this book.

ALMOND FLOUR • Almond flour is also found in most grocery stores' baking aisles, or can be ordered online. Look for blanched almond flour, which has the almond skins removed before processing.

HAZELNUT FLOUR • Hazelnut flour is found in most grocery stores' baking aisles, or can be ordered online. If you can't find it, you can pulse skinned hazelnuts in a food processor until finely ground.

Leavenings

BAKING POWDER • I use non-aluminum baking powder when I bake, as brands with aluminum can give off the taste of metal. Baking powder can expire; to check if your baking powder is still potent, add a spoonful of it to a cup of hot water. If it bubbles, it is still good to use.

BAKING SODA • In order for baking soda to rise, it needs to be paired with an acidic ingredient, such as buttermilk, sour cream, yogurt, vinegar, coffee, molasses, brown sugar, or pumpkin. You can check baking soda for freshness the same way you would check baking powder.

Nuts

I usually toast nuts as soon as I purchase them and then store them in the freezer, as nuts can turn rancid. To toast nuts: Adjust an oven rack to the middle position and preheat the oven to 350°F [180°C]. Line a sheet pan with parchment paper and place the nuts in the prepared pan in a single layer. Bake for 5 to 10 minutes, until the nuts darken and become fragrant. Let them cool, and then store them in a plastic freezer bag in the freezer for up to 1 month.

Chocolate

BITTERSWEET/SEMISWEET CHOCOLATE • When shopping for semi-sweet and bittersweet bar chocolate to use in baking, look for bars that contain between 35 and 60 percent cacao, and don't use

anything over 70 percent, as this can alter the taste and texture of the recipe. (*Bittersweet* and *semisweet* can be confusing terms, as both can mean chocolate with a cacao percentage of anywhere from 35 to 99 percent.) Most recipes in this book call for semisweet chocolate.

When melting chocolate: Chop the bar into fine pieces. This will help the chocolate melt more quickly and evenly and will give it less opportunity to burn. Make sure that there is no water in your bowl when melting, or on your knife and spatula, as contact with water can cause the chocolate to seize and turn grainy. Adding a tablespoon or two of hot water to the seized chocolate and then stirring it can sometimes save it.

To melt chocolate in the microwave: Place the chopped chocolate in a microwave-safe bowl and microwave the chocolate on medium heat for 1 minute, then stop and stir the chocolate. Continue to microwave the chocolate in 20-second intervals, stirring after each one, until the chocolate is almost completely smooth. Remove the bowl from the microwave and then stir until completely smooth.

CACAO NIBS • Cacao nibs have a complex, bitter flavor and a crunchy texture.

CHOCOLATE CHIPS • Chocolate chips have less cacao than bar chocolate, which allows them to hold their shape when melted. This does mean, however, that they are not always a good substitution for melted bar chocolate in a recipe; they will not melt as quickly or as smoothly. Have I, in a pinch, used chocolate chips for bar chocolate? Yes. Have I regretted it? About half the time.

COCOA POWDER • There are two kinds of cocoa powder: Dutch-process and natural. Dutch-process cocoa is treated; it is washed with an alkaline solution that neutralizes its acids, giving it a mellower, nutty flavor and a richer color. Natural cocoa powder is left as is, and is a very acidic, sharp powder. The recipes in this book all call for Dutch-process cocoa powder.

WHITE CHOCOLATE • White chocolate is made from cocoa butter. Not all white chocolate is created equal, so use a brand you trust when baking with it. White chocolate melts more quickly than dark chocolate, so be sure to stir it more frequently than you would dark chocolate, especially when using the microwave to melt it down. White chocolate chips, meanwhile, do not melt well.

Vanilla

VANILLA BEANS • To use a vanilla bean: Use a sharp knife to split the bean lengthwise, then scrape the seeds out of the bean with the dull side of the knife or a spoon. Use the seeds in the recipe as called for. The leftover pod can be dried and then finely ground in a food processor to make a vanilla bean powder. Vanilla bean powder can be stirred into coffee, sprinkled on top of baked goods (such as muffins and scones), or used to make vanilla sugar or salt.

VANILLA EXTRACT • All the recipes in this book use pure vanilla extract, and I don't recommend using artificial vanilla, as the taste is, well, artificial.

EQUIPMENT

Measuring Equipment

DIGITAL SCALE • A digital scale will ensure that your ingredients are measured correctly. Throughout this book, I have weights listed for most ingredients. I have not included small measurements that are less than 4 tablespoons. A digital scale can also be used for portioning out cookie dough and dividing cake batter evenly between pans.

MEASURING CUPS AND SPOONS • Dry measuring cups measure dry ingredients. I use metal cups that come in these sizes: ¼ cup, ⅓ cup, ½ cup, and 1 cup. I use metal measuring spoons for teaspoon and tablespoon measures: ¼ teaspoon, ½ teaspoon, 1 teaspoon, and 1 tablespoon. For liquids and semisolids, I use glass measuring cups with pourable spouts and measurements marked along the side of the cup.

Tools

BENCH SCRAPER • A bench scraper is a great tool to use for so many things, from transferring ingredients to lifting dough off the counter, cutting dough, and cleaning the work surface.

FOOD PROCESSOR • I use a food processor for pulverizing nuts and grating carrots quickly.

HEAVY-DUTY STAND MIXER • If you do a lot of baking, I highly recommend investing in a stand mixer for both convenience and speed. The recipes in this book call for one, but a handheld mixer or sturdy wooden spoon can be substituted.

INSTANT-READ THERMOMETER • An instant-read thermometer is an essential tool and is especially useful when making caramel. As its name suggests, it tells the temperature instantly, so you have a better chance of making your confections perfectly.

KITCHEN SCISSORS • Kitchen scissors have many functions, such as cutting parchment paper and pastry bag tips, as well as snipping dough.

KITCHEN TORCH • I use my kitchen torch to caramelize sugar, brown meringues, and toast marshmallows.

MICROWAVE OVEN • A microwave oven is a useful alternative to a double boiler for melting butter and chocolate and also works well to heat milk.

OFFSET SPATULA • Offset spatulas are used for spreading batter evenly and icing cookies and cakes. I use both large and small ones, and prefer them with a rounded edge over a straight edge.

OVEN THERMOMETER • Many ovens are not properly calibrated, and this can greatly affect the outcome of your baked good. I keep an inexpensive oven thermometer hanging on the middle rack of my oven.

PARCHMENT PAPER • I use parchment paper for lining sheet pans when baking and as a sling for easy removal when making quick breads and bars. I like to buy parchment paper from a restaurant supply store, where the sheets come precut and lie flat.

PASTRY BRUSHES • Pastry brushes have so many uses—glazing, coating, and brushing away crumbs and excess flour. I use a natural-bristle brush; I've found they work much better than silicone, although they need to be replaced more frequently.

PORTION SCOOP • Portion scoops are a great way to scoop batter, helping ensure consistent and even shapes. They are not essential, but I highly recommend them. Vollrath makes a reliable scoop that doesn't break easily.

RULER • Rulers are useful for measuring when cutting dough. I have an 18 in [46 cm] ruler that works perfectly.

SHEET PAN • I use medium-weight half sheet pans (12 by 16 in [30.5 by 40.5 cm] with a 1 in [2.5 cm] rim), unless otherwise noted.

SILICONE SPATULA • Spatulas are an essential kitchen tool with many uses: folding, smoothing, stirring, mixing, and scraping, just to name a few.

SKEWERS • I use wooden skewers for testing when bars and brownies are done. A toothpick can also be used.

WIRE COOLING RACK • Cooling racks help the bottom of baked goods stay crisp and also help speed up cooling times.

WIRE WHISK • I use whisks for many kitchen tasks, such as beating eggs and combining dry ingredients.

ZESTER • A Microplane zester comes in handy when a recipe calls for freshly grated nutmeg or ginger, or the zest of an orange or lemon.

1

"... the rooms were very still while the pages were softly turned, and the winter sunshine crept in to touch the bright heads and serious faces with a Christmas greeting."

–LOUISA MAY ALCOTT, *LITTLE WOMEN*

Morning Breads and Pastries

Classic Cinnamon Rolls

If I am being completely honest, I often look no further than this recipe for holiday baking. I've never had anyone be disappointed by a warm pan of cinnamon rolls emerging from the oven, and my family requests these swirly buns for almost every celebration. This recipe also appeared in my first book and has acquired quite a following after taking first place in a cinnamon roll bake-off on The Kitchn website. I've included it again because it is my absolute favorite, but I have added a few filling variations and new ways to shape the dough.

	FILLING	ICING	
All-purpose flour, for dusting	½ cup [100 g] light brown sugar	8 tablespoons [1 stick or 113 g] unsalted butter, at room temperature	1 teaspoon pure vanilla extract
1 recipe Sweet Dough, page 76	1 tablespoon ground cinnamon		¼ teaspoon salt
	Pinch salt	4 oz [113 g] cream cheese, at room temperature	1 cup [120 g] confectioners' sugar
	2 tablespoons unsalted butter, melted and cooled		

Flour a work surface and knead the cold dough ten to twelve times. Shape the dough into a ball, cover the top lightly with flour, cover with a tea towel or plastic wrap, and let the dough come just to room temperature. • Grease a 9 by 13 in [23 by 33 cm] baking pan; if desired, line it with a parchment sling (see page 16).

continued

25

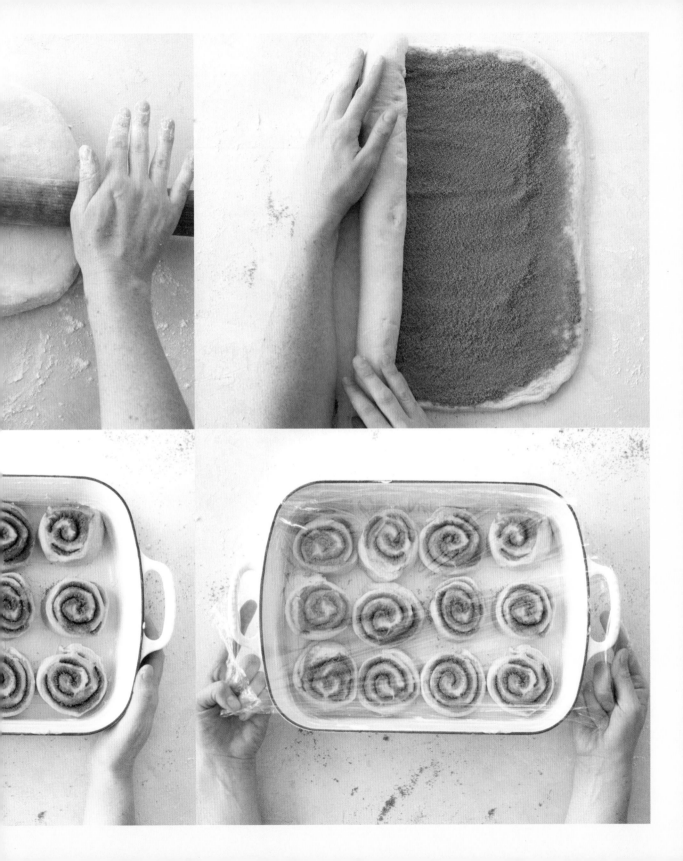

FOR THE FILLING

In a small bowl, mix together the brown sugar, cinnamon, and salt. • Lightly flour your work surface and roll the dough into a 12 by 16 in [30.5 by 40.5 cm] rectangle. Brush the dough with the melted butter and sprinkle the cinnamon-sugar mixture evenly over the top, pressing it lightly into the butter so it adheres. Starting at a long side, roll the dough into a tight cylinder. Pinch the seam gently to seal it and position the dough seam-side down. Use scissors or a sharp knife to cut the dough into twelve equal pieces. Transfer the pieces to the prepared pan and place them cut-side up, tucking the tail of each cinnamon roll underneath itself. *See how-to photos pages 26–27.* Cover the pan loosely with plastic wrap and let the dough rise until doubled in size, 1 to 1½ hours. (Rolls can also do a slow rise in the refrigerator overnight; see Make It Early, page 31.) • Adjust an oven rack to the middle position and preheat the oven to 350°F [180°C]. Remove the plastic wrap and bake the cinnamon rolls for 27 to 32 minutes, rotating the pan halfway through, until the rolls are light golden brown.

FOR THE ICING

While the rolls are baking, in the bowl of a stand mixer fitted with a paddle, beat the butter and cream cheese on medium speed until smooth and creamy. Add the vanilla and salt and mix on low speed until combined. Add the confectioners' sugar and mix on low speed until combined. Scrape down the sides of the bowl and mix on medium speed until the icing is light and fluffy, 3 to 4 minutes. • Transfer the pan of rolls to a wire rack and let cool for 5 minutes. Using an offset spatula or table knife, apply a thin layer of the icing, using about one-third of the mixture. Let the rolls cool for another 15 to 20 minutes. Top with the rest of the icing and serve. Cinnamon rolls are best eaten the same day they are made.

NOTES

Depending on your preferred size, the dough can be cut into eight, ten, or twelve pieces. Add a few minutes to the baking time for larger-size buns. • I like my cinnamon rolls super soft with a gooey center, so I put a thin layer of the icing over them almost right out of the oven. The icing melts into the warm rolls, eliminating any hard corners or edges. If you prefer a little crispy crunch to your cinnamon rolls, you can wait until they have cooled and then top them with all the icing.

continued

FOR OVERNIGHT CINNAMON ROLLS

Prepare the rolls—roll out the dough, fill them, roll them up, cut them, and place them in the prepared pan—but do not let them rise for 1½ hours as stated in the recipe. Instead, cover them loosely with plastic wrap and refrigerate for at least 8 hours and up to 18 hours. When ready to bake, preheat the oven and let the rolls sit at room temperature (still covered in plastic wrap) for 30 to 45 minutes. Bake as directed (they make take slightly longer to bake).

HOW TO MAKE THE ROLLS OVER A FEW DAYS

Two days before serving, make the Sweet Dough, letting it rise overnight in the fridge, as directed. The day before serving, form the buns (roll out and cut) and let rise again overnight in the fridge. The morning of, let the buns come to room temperature on the counter as directed, and then bake.

Extra Filling

Using an offset spatula, spread 5 tablespoons [70 g] unsalted, room-temperature butter evenly across the dough, leaving a border. Mix together ⅔ cup [135 g] light brown sugar, 2 tablespoons ground cinnamon, and a pinch of salt, and sprinkle over the dough, pressing it into the butter so it adheres.

Cinnamon Rolls with Sugared Cranberries

Prepare and roll out the dough as directed, and spread the regular cinnamon roll filling over the dough. Dollop ⅓ cup [100 g] Cranberry Jam (page 202) over the sugar and cinnamon mixture. Roll, cut, and bake the dough as directed in the main recipe. After icing the cinnamon rolls, sprinkle with Sugared Cranberries (page 80).

31

continued

Cinnamon Braid

In a small bowl, mix together ½ cup [100 g] light brown sugar, 1 tablespoon ground cinnamon, and a pinch of salt. Lightly flour your work surface and roll out ½ recipe of Sweet Dough (page 76) into a 16 by 14 in [40.5 by 35.5 cm] rectangle. Brush the dough with 2 tablespoons melted, unsalted butter and sprinkle the cinnamon-sugar mixture evenly over the top, pressing it lightly into the butter so it adheres. Starting at a long side, roll the dough into a tight cylinder. Pinch the seam gently to seal it and position the dough seam-side down. Chill the log on a parchment-lined sheet pan for 15 minutes. Using a bench scraper, cut the log in half lengthwise, then place the pieces cut-side up next to each other and twist the pieces together, making a "braid." Twist the log into a circle, tucking the end under the braid. *See how-to photos, facing page.* Cover the braid loosely with plastic wrap on the sheet pan and let rise until doubled in size, about 1 hour. Bake in a 350°F [180°C] oven for 20 to 28 minutes, until golden brown and set in the middle. Let cool on a wire rack for 5 minutes, then cover with icing (see main recipe), if desired.

Giant Cinnamon Roll

In a small bowl, combine ½ cup [100 g] light brown sugar, 1 tablespoon ground cinnamon, and a pinch of salt. Lightly flour your work surface and roll ½ recipe Sweet Dough (page 76) into a 14 by 12 in [35.5 by 30.5 cm] rectangle. Brush the dough with 2 tablespoons melted butter and sprinkle the cinnamon-sugar mixture evenly over the top, pressing it lightly into the butter so it adheres. Cut the dough into seven equal strips, each strip measuring 2 by 12 in [5 by 30.5 cm]. Roll the first strip into a tight coil. Wrap the next strip around the coil, winding it completely around. Repeat with each remaining strip, until you have a giant coil of cinnamon roll. *See how-to photos, facing page.* Place the dough into a greased and lined 8 in [20 cm] cake pan (see page 16). Cover the cinnamon roll loosely with plastic wrap and let rise until doubled in size, about 1 hour. Bake in a 350°F [180°C] oven for 20 to 28 minutes, until golden brown and set in the middle. Let cool on a wire rack for 5 minutes, then cover with icing (see main recipe), if desired.

Nutella Star Bread

There are many different ways to twist and shape bread, and this might be my favorite. Of course, in the long, ancient history of bread, this pretty little star is nothing new, and I've found hundreds of variations of it over the years. I first made this bread for *Artisan Bread in Five Minutes a Day* (where I contribute recipes each month), using their no-knead brioche dough as the base. I loved it so much I experimented with my own Sweet Dough (page 76), with great results. This star calls for a half recipe of dough, but the filling can be doubled to make two stars, if desired.

½ recipe Sweet Dough (page 76)

All-purpose flour, for dusting

¾ cup [225 g] Nutella

Egg wash (see page 16)

Sanding sugar, for sprinkling

Line a sheet pan with parchment paper. • Divide the dough into four equal pieces. Roll the pieces into balls, cover with plastic wrap, and let rest for 10 minutes. • Generously flour your work surface and roll out all the dough balls into 10 in [25 cm] circles. Place one of the circles on the prepared pan, and spread one-third of the Nutella over the top, leaving a ½ in [12 mm] border. Place another dough circle on top of the first circle, and spread another third of the Nutella on top. Repeat with one more dough circle, then place the final dough circle on top. Chill the dough for 15 minutes. • Remove the dough from the refrigerator and place a 2½ in [6 cm] biscuit cutter (or other round object) in the center of the circle, but don't press it down to cut the dough. Use a bench scraper to cut the circle into sixteen equal strips (starting at the biscuit cutter and slicing out to the edge of the dough circle), cutting through all the layers.

37

continued

Take two adjacent wedges of dough and twist them away from each other twice. Pinch the ends of the pairs of strips firmly together. Repeat around the whole circle to create the star (you should end up with eight points). Remove the biscuit cutter from the center of the star. *See how-to photos, facing page.* • Cover the star gently with plastic wrap and let rise for 45 minutes to 1 hour until a bit puffy. • Adjust an oven rack to the middle position and preheat the oven to 350°F [180°C]. Brush the dough star with egg wash and sprinkle with the sanding sugar. Repinch the star tips together if needed. Bake for 20 to 28 minutes, until golden brown. Star bread is best eaten the day it's made.

NOTE

The Nutella can sometimes be hard to spread across the dough. I've found chilling the round dough circles for 10 minutes before assembling helps it go on a little easier.

VARIATIONS

Jam-Filled Star

Replace the Nutella with your favorite flavor of jam.

Cinnamon-Sugar Star

Replace the Nutella with the filling for the Cinnamon Braid (page 32).

Morning Buns

These buns are (of course) inspired by the famous morning buns created at Tartine. On my only visit to San Francisco, I was able to try one of these perfect buns—orange and cinnamon and sugar and butter all wrapped up in a flaky dough. I've tried to re-create the buns here using my Cheater's Croissant Dough (page 70), and I must say I am happy with the results. The orange and cinnamon scents that waft from the oven as they bake will fill your whole home with cheer. For the best flavor, let the buns rise overnight in the refrigerator.

1 cup [200 g] granulated sugar, plus more for coating the muffin pan	2 tablespoons orange zest 1 tablespoon ground cinnamon Pinch salt	All-purpose flour, for dusting 1 recipe Cheater's Croissant Dough (page 70)	3 tablespoons unsalted butter, melted, plus more for greasing the muffin pan

Generously butter the insides and top of a twelve-cup standard muffin pan and coat each muffin cup well with granulated sugar, tapping out any excess. • In a small bowl, mix together ½ cup [100 g] of the sugar, the orange zest, cinnamon, and salt. • Generously flour your work surface and roll out the croissant dough into a 10 by 24 in [25 by 60 cm] rectangle. Brush the dough with the melted butter, then sprinkle the sugar mixture evenly over the dough, gently pressing it into the butter to adhere. Starting at a long side, roll up the dough into a tight cylinder and position the dough seam-side down (as with the Classic Cinnamon Rolls, page 26). Cut the dough into twelve equal pieces, each measuring about 2 in [5 cm] wide. Transfer the pieces to the prepared muffin pan and place them cut-side down. Cover the pan loosely with plastic wrap and let the dough rise until doubled in size and puffy (it should act similarly to a marshmallow when pressed), 2 to 2½ hours. (The buns can also do a slow rise in the refrigerator overnight; see Make It Early [page 43]).

continued

Adjust an oven rack to the middle position and preheat the oven to 400°F [200°C]. • Remove the plastic wrap and gently press down on the top of each bun with a lightly greased spatula. Place a sheet pan on a lower oven rack (this will help catch any drips); do not place the sheet pan directly under the muffin pan on the same rack or it will interfere with baking. Bake the buns for 15 minutes, then carefully press down on the tops of the buns again with a spatula. Rotate the pan and continue baking until the buns are golden brown, 10 to 15 minutes more. • While the buns are baking, fill a pie plate or bowl with the remaining ½ cup [100 g] of granulated sugar. Remove the pan from the oven and immediately flip the hot buns onto a sheet pan lined with parchment paper. Using tongs, pick up one bun at a time and evenly coat it in the bowl of sugar. Repeat with the remaining buns, placing them on a wire rack to cool. Morning buns are best eaten the same day they are made.

MAKE IT EARLY

FOR OVERNIGHT MORNING BUNS

Prepare the buns (roll the dough, fill them, roll them up, cut them, and place them in the prepared pan), but do not let them rise for 2 hours as stated in the main recipe. Instead, cover them loosely with plastic and refrigerate for at least 8 hours and up to 18 hours. When ready to bake, preheat the oven and let the buns sit at room temperature (still covered in plastic wrap) until puffy, 1½ to 2 hours. Bake as directed.

VARIATION

Panettone Morning Buns

Add 1 tablespoon of lemon zest to the filling, along with 1 cup [170 g] of mixed dried and/or candied fruit: cranberries, Candied Orange Peels (page 201), golden raisins, dried pineapple, dried apricots, and dried cherries are all good options.

Cranberries and Cream Danish

Cinnamon rolls are my top of the pops, but Danish runs a close second place—all those beautiful, flaky layers, and then a pool of fruit and cream right in the center. If you're not feeling up for making cranberry jam, it can be replaced with canned whole-berry cranberry sauce, Lemon Curd (page 208), or any jam flavor your heart desires. I use my Cheater's Croissant Dough (page 70) here rather than my Easy Danish Dough (page 74) to ensure extra flaky layers.

CREAM CHEESE FILLING

4 oz [113 g] cream cheese, at room temperature

3 tablespoons granulated sugar

Pinch salt

1 teaspoon pure vanilla extract

ASSEMBLY

All-purpose flour, for dusting

½ recipe Cheater's Croissant Dough (page 70)

Egg wash (see page 16)

Cranberry Jam (page 202)

Granulated sugar, for sprinkling

FOR THE CREAM CHEESE FILLING

In the bowl of a stand mixer fitted with a paddle, beat the cream cheese on medium speed until smooth. Add the sugar and salt and beat again on medium speed until the mixture is completely smooth. Scrape down the sides, add the vanilla, and beat on low speed until combined. Chill the mixture until ready to use. The filling can be refrigerated in an airtight container up to 2 days ahead.

continued

TO ASSEMBLE

Line two sheet pans with parchment paper. Flour a work surface and roll the dough into a 10 by 18 in [25 by 46 cm] rectangle, flouring as needed so the dough doesn't stick. Use a pastry cutter to trim off any rough edges of the rectangle and discard them. • Cut the dough vertically into ten 1 by 18 in [2.5 by 46 cm] strips. Place the cut strips on the prepared pans, cover with plastic wrap, and refrigerate for 15 minutes. • Hold one end of a dough strip in place with one hand. Using your other hand, twist the strip several times. Curl the twisted strip around itself into a spiral shape. Tuck the loose end of the strip underneath the spiral and place the shaped dough on a prepared sheet pan. Repeat with the remaining dough strips, spacing the spirals 2 in [5 cm] apart. *See how-to photos, facing page.* Cover lightly with the plastic wrap and let rise at room temperature until puffy (it should act similarly to a marshmallow when pressed), about 2 hours. (Danish can also do a slow rise in the refrigerator overnight, see Make It Early, following.) • Adjust the oven racks to the upper-middle and lower-middle positions and preheat the oven to 400°F [200°C]. • Just before baking, gently press the center of each dough spiral to make a spot for the fillings, 1 to 2 in [2.5 to 5 cm] wide, trying to not push on the rest of the dough. Lightly brush the dough with the egg wash and then place a teaspoon of cranberry jam and a teaspoon of cream cheese filling in the center of each piece. Sprinkle the exposed dough with a generous amount of sugar. Bake for 10 minutes, then rotate the pans and bake for 8 to 10 minutes more, until the pastries are golden brown. • Transfer the sheet pans to a wire rack and let cool to room temperature. Danish are best eaten the same day they are made.

MAKE IT EARLY

FOR OVERNIGHT DANISH

Prepare the dough spirals, but do not let them rise for 2 hours as stated above. Instead, cover them loosely with plastic wrap and refrigerate for at least 8 hours and up to 18 hours. When ready to bake, preheat the oven and let the dough sit at room temperature (still covered in plastic wrap) until puffy, 1½ to 2 hours. Bake as directed.

Cranberries and Cream Danish

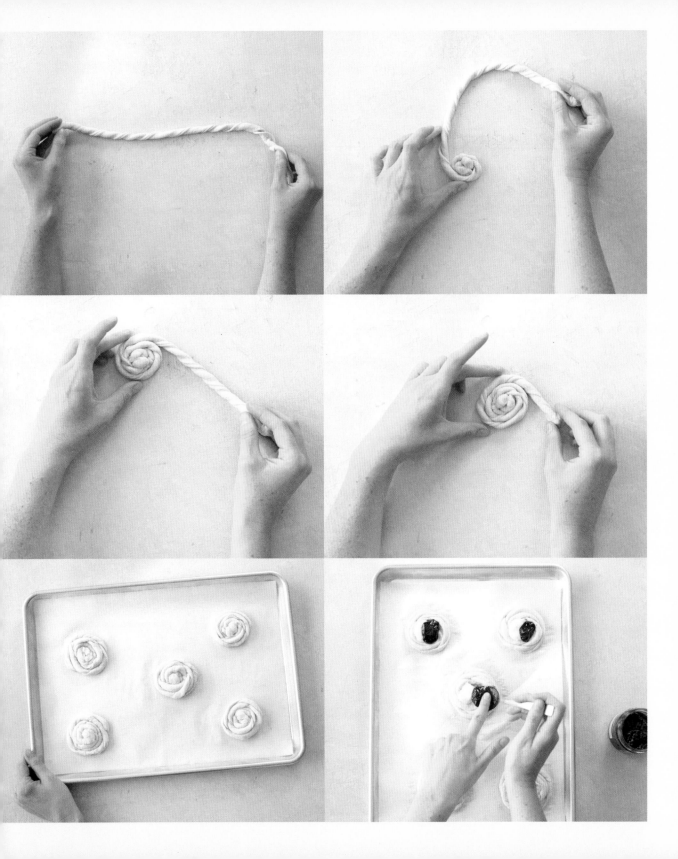

Pear-Almond Danish Braid

Pears, almond, and a rich, flaky crust—this braid never fails to impress. Although at first glance it may appear complicated to create, the steps to forming the braid are actually a snap.

PEAR FILLING

2 large Bartlett pears, peeled and sliced into ½ in [12 mm] pieces

¼ cup [50 g] granulated sugar

1½ teaspoon almond extract

Pinch salt

ASSEMBLY

All-purpose flour, for dusting

½ recipe Easy Danish Dough (page 74)

Egg wash (see page 16)

ICING

¾ cup [90 g] confectioners' sugar

2 to 4 tablespoons [30 to 60 g] water

1 tablespoon unsalted butter, melted

½ teaspoon pure vanilla extract

½ cup [50 g] toasted sliced almonds, for sprinkling

50

FOR THE FILLING

In a small bowl, combine the pears, granulated sugar, almond extract, and salt.

TO ASSEMBLE

Line a sheet pan with parchment paper. On a lightly floured work surface, roll the dough into a 10 by 14 in [25 by 35.5 cm] rectangle, using enough flour so the dough doesn't stick to the surface or the rolling pin.

continued

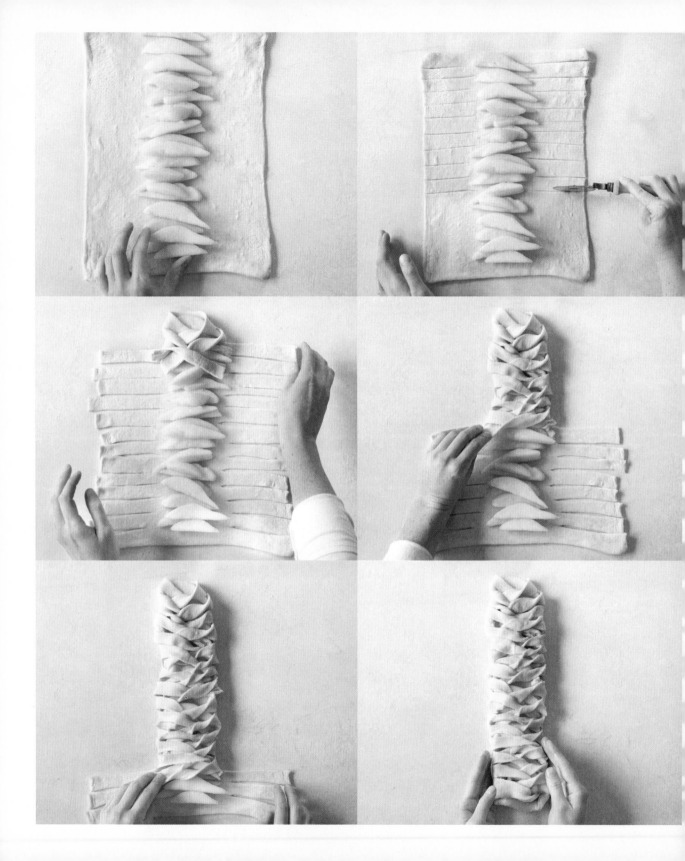

Transfer the dough to the prepared pan with a long side facing you and arrange the pears down the center of the dough (any leftover pear juice in the bowl can be used in place of the water in the icing, if desired). • Working from the filling out to the edge of the dough, carefully cut ½ in [12 mm] thick strips of dough (a pastry cutter works best here), doing your best to make the strips even and equal on both sides. • Starting with the top two pieces, gently twist, then cross the pieces over the top of the filling. Continue the same motion of twisting the pieces and crossing them all the way down the braid. When you get to end of the braid, tuck the loose ends underneath the braid (this way, they won't pop out when baking). *See how-to photos, facing page.* Cover the braid loosely with plastic wrap and let rise until puffy (it should act similarly to a marshmallow when pressed), about 1½ hours. (The braid can also do a slow rise in the refrigerator overnight; see Make It Early, following.) • Adjust an oven rack to the middle position and preheat the oven to 350°F [180°C]. Lightly brush the braid with the egg wash and bake for 25 to 30 minutes, until golden brown. Transfer the sheet pan to a wire rack and let cool slightly.

FOR THE ICING

While the braid is baking and cooling, in a medium bowl, whisk together the confectioners' sugar, 2 tablespoons of the water, the melted butter, and vanilla until smooth. Add more water, 1 tablespoon at a time, to thin the icing to your preferred consistency. Drizzle the warm braid with the icing and sprinkle the toasted almonds across the top. The braid is best eaten the same day it's made.

MAKE IT EARLY

FOR AN OVERNIGHT DANISH BRAID

Prepare the braid, but do not let it rise for 1½ hours as stated above. Instead, cover it loosely with plastic wrap and refrigerate for at least 8 hours and up to 18 hours. When ready to bake, preheat the oven and let the braid sit at room temperature (still covered in plastic wrap) until puffy, 1½ to 2 hours. Bake as directed.

Coffee-Cardamom Monkey Bread

Whenever my mom made monkey bread for Christmas morning or Easter Sunday, my siblings and I would anxiously pace in front of the oven door until it emerged, the caramel bubbling and the dough balls busting out of the top. We would hold our breath, waiting for the big flip; my mom would gear up with both oven mitts and close her eyes in a silent prayer as she turned the pan over onto a plate. Would it fall in one piece? We didn't care. She would yell at us to wait for it to cool as we burned our fingers on the hot caramel, grabbing for any stray bites that refused to stay put. She'd limit our intake to three pieces each, but we'd creep back in the kitchen when her back was turned, sneaking so many more.

DOUGH

½ cup [120 g] whole milk

¼ cup [60 g] sour cream

1 large egg plus 2 large egg yolks

2 tablespoons honey

1 teaspoon pure vanilla extract

3 cups plus 1 tablespoon [435 g] all-purpose flour

¼ cup [50 g] granulated sugar

2 teaspoons instant yeast

1½ teaspoons salt

4 tablespoons [57 g] unsalted butter, at room temperature, cut into 1 in [2.5 cm] pieces

COATING

6 tablespoons [84 g] unsalted butter, melted

¾ cup [150 g] granulated sugar

1 teaspoon ground cardamom

¼ teaspoon fine sea salt

COFFEE CARAMEL

½ cup [120 g] strong, freshly brewed coffee

3 tablespoons corn syrup

8 tablespoons [1 stick or 113 g] unsalted butter

¾ cup [150 g] light brown sugar

¼ cup [50 g] granulated sugar

½ teaspoon salt

1 tablespoon Kahlúa (optional)

2 teaspoons pure vanilla extract

In a medium bowl or liquid measuring cup, mix together the milk, sour cream, egg, yolks, honey, and vanilla. • In the bowl of a stand mixer fitted with a dough hook, mix together the flour, granulated sugar, yeast, and salt on low speed. Add the wet mixture to the dry and mix on low speed until combined. The dough will be shaggy at first, and you may need to scrape down the hook. Knead on medium speed for 6 to 8 minutes, scraping down the sides of the bowl as needed, until the dough is smooth and elastic. • Add the butter one piece at a time, mixing on low speed until completely combined (this may take a few minutes). Increase the speed to medium-low and knead for a few minutes more, until all the butter is incorporated and the dough is smooth. If the dough is sticking to the sides of the bowl, add 1 tablespoon more of flour and knead until incorporated. Place the dough in a large, greased bowl. Cover with plastic wrap and let rise in a warm, draft-free area until it has puffed up and is almost double in size, 1½ to 2 hours. Dough can be used immediately or refrigerated for up to 18 hours. • When ready to bake, spray a 10 in [25 cm] Bundt or tube pan or one 9 by 4 by 4 in [23 by 10 by 10 cm] Pullman pan generously with nonstick cooking spray. Using a bench scraper or scissors, divide the dough into 1½ in [4 cm] pieces (thirty-six to forty total) and roll them into balls.

FOR THE COATING

Pour the melted butter into a small bowl. In a medium bowl, whisk together the granulated sugar, ground cardamom, and salt. Working with a few at a time, cover the dough balls with the melted butter, then toss them in the cardamom sugar to coat. Place the balls into the prepared pan in two rows (the bottom row of sugary balls will end up as the top when the bread is flipped). Cover the pan with plastic wrap and set on a sheet pan lined with parchment. Let rise in a warm place until doubled in size, about 1 hour. (Monkey bread can also do a slow rise in the refrigerator overnight; see Make It Early, page 56.) • Adjust an oven rack to the middle position and preheat the oven to 350°F [180°C].

55

Morning Breads and Pastries

continued

While the dough is rising, in a medium sauce-pan over medium heat, combine the coffee, corn syrup, butter, brown and granulated sugars, and salt. Bring the mixture to a boil, stirring often, until the sugar is dissolved. Let simmer until thickened, 6 to 8 minutes. Stir in the Kahlúa, if using, and vanilla off the heat and let cool slightly. Pour the caramel over the risen dough. • Place the filled pan in the oven with the prepared sheet pan underneath (this will help catch any caramel that may bubble over).

Bake until puffed and golden, 35 to 40 minutes (the bread should register at least 190°F [88°C] on an instant-read thermometer). If baking in a Pullman pan, the three layers may take more time, 42 to 45 minutes. If the monkey bread is browning too fast at any point, cover the pan with aluminum foil. Let the bread cool in the pan on a wire rack for 8 to 10 minutes, then invert onto a platter. Serve the monkey bread warm; it's best eaten the same day it's made.

MAKE IT EARLY

FOR OVERNIGHT MONKEY BREAD

Prepare the Coffee-Cardamom Monkey Bread, but do not let it rise for 1 hour as stated above. Instead, cover the pan loosely with plastic wrap and refrigerate for at least 8 hours and up to

18 hours. Preheat the oven and let the bread sit at room temperature (still covered) for 45 minutes to 1 hour. Bake as directed.

VARIATION

Cinnamon Sugar Monkey Bread

Omit the cardamom from the coating and replace it with 1 tablespoon ground cinnamon. Omit the coffee and Kahlúa from the Coffee Caramel.

Powdered Sugar Donuts

Mini donuts! With all the options for fancy, over-the-top, Instagram-able donuts, I often forget the simple pleasure of a tiny donut coated in sugar. In the past, these small circles were enjoyed at some kind of amusement park or fair—a bag purchased on the way out after a long day of walking for miles and spending way too much money on food already. Now they can be made right at home. I highly recommend eating the donuts fresh and warm, as soon as they are able to be handled.

DONUTS

½ cup [120 g] whole milk

¼ cup [60 g] sour cream

1 large egg plus 2 large egg yolks, at room temperature

2 tablespoons honey

1 tablespoon pure vanilla extract

3 cups [426 g] all-purpose flour, plus more for dusting

¼ cup [50 g] granulated sugar

1 tablespoon instant dry yeast

1½ teaspoons salt

8 tablespoons [1 stick or 113 g] unsalted butter, at room temperature and cut into 1 in [2.5 cm] pieces

SUGAR COATING

1 cup [120 g] confectioners' sugar

1½ teaspoons ground nutmeg

ASSEMBLY

Canola oil, for frying (enough to fill a medium to large Dutch oven 4 in [10 cm] from the top)

3 tablespoons unsalted butter, melted

FOR THE DONUTS

In a medium bowl or liquid measuring cup, mix together the milk, sour cream, egg, yolks, honey, and vanilla. • In the bowl of a stand mixer fitted with a dough hook, mix together the flour, granulated sugar, yeast, and salt on low speed.

continued

Add the wet mixture to the dry and mix on low speed until combined. The dough will be shaggy at first, and you may need to scrape down the hook. Knead the dough on medium speed for 6 to 8 minutes, scraping down the sides of the bowl as needed, until the dough is smooth and elastic. The dough will start to pull away from the sides, although it will still be sticky. Add the butter one piece at time, mixing on low speed until completely combined (this will take a few minutes). • Increase the speed to medium-low and knead for 2 to 3 minutes more, until all the butter is incorporated and the dough is smooth. If the dough is sticking to the sides of the bowl, add 1 tablespoon more of flour and knead until incorporated. • Place the dough inside a large, greased bowl. Cover with plastic wrap and let rise in a warm, draft-free area until it has puffed up and is almost double in size, 1½ to 2 hours. Refrigerate for 2 hours and up to overnight. • When ready to bake, move the dough to a lightly floured work surface. • Cut two dozen 5 in [12 cm] square pieces of parchment paper, then arrange them on two sheet pans and lightly grease them with cooking spray. (The parchment paper will help the donuts keep their shape when transferring them to the hot oil—the parchment will go into the oil with the donuts.) • Using a 2 in [5 cm] biscuit cutter, cut the dough into rounds, and then use a smaller cutter to cut a hole in the center of each dough round. Transfer the donuts to the prepared sheet pan; place two donuts on each piece of cut parchment paper, with some space in between them for rising (alternatively, you can cut smaller pieces of parchment for each donut, but I didn't have the patience). Scraps of dough can be re-rolled and used one more time, although those donuts won't turn out quite as pretty. • Cover the donuts with greased plastic wrap and let rise in a warm, draft-free spot for 1½ hours; the donuts should almost double in height. (Donuts can also do a slow rise in the refrigerator overnight; see Make It Early, facing page.)

FOR THE SUGAR COATING
Meanwhile, in a medium bowl, whisk together the confectioners' sugar and the nutmeg.

TO ASSEMBLE
When the donuts are ready to fry, heat the oil in a large Dutch oven, wok, or deep fryer to 365°F [185°C]. Place two donuts (on their paper) in a wire basket skimmer and gently drop them into the hot oil. Fry a few donuts at a time, being careful not to crowd them. Use tongs to pluck out the papers. Let the donuts cook for about 1 minute, until golden brown on the bottom, then use the skimmer to flip them over to the uncooked side. Fry again for about 1 minute, monitoring the oil temperature and adjusting the heat as needed. Use the skimmer to transfer the donuts to a wire rack set over paper towels and let cool for 1 to 2 minutes. Repeat with the remaining donuts. Brush the just-warm donuts with the melted butter. Toss the donuts in the sugar coating until all sides are completely coated. For extra pretty donuts, sift the remaining powdered sugar in the bowl over the tops of the donuts. Donuts are best eaten immediately.

FOR OVERNIGHT DONUTS

Prepare the donuts (cut them into rounds and cut out the center hole), but do not let them rise for 1½ hours as stated in the main recipe. Instead, cover the pan loosely with plastic wrap and refrigerate for 8 hours and up to 18 hours.

When ready to bake, let the donuts sit at room temperature (still covered in plastic wrap) for 1 to 1½ hours, until doubled in size. Heat the oil and cook as directed.

Streusel Coffee Cake

I have always loved coffee cake, with its tender cake base, topping of streusel, and thick coat of icing. It's hard to find a perfect piece of it, though—all the streusel and icing can cause its flavor profile to be just too *sweet*. After much testing, I found using my white cake base gives it a tender crumb, and a swirl of cream cheese lends some needed tang. I also highly recommend the lemon variation during the post-holiday months.

COFFEE CAKE

1 cup [240 g] whole milk, at room temperature

1 scant cup [210 g] large egg whites (from 6 or 7 eggs), at room temperature (see note, page 65)

½ cup [120 g] Crème Fraîche (page 205) or sour cream, at room temperature

1 tablespoon pure vanilla extract

2¾ cups [391 g] all-purpose flour

2 cups [400 g] granulated sugar

4 teaspoons baking powder

1 teaspoon salt

1 cup [2 sticks or 227 g] unsalted butter, at room temperature, cut into 1 in [2.5 cm] pieces

CREAM CHEESE FILLING

4 oz [113 g] cream cheese, at room temperature

2 tablespoons granulated sugar

1½ cups [188 g] Streusel (page 203)

ICING

1½ cups [180 g] confectioners' sugar

2 to 4 tablespoons [30 to 60 g] water

1 tablespoon unsalted butter, melted

½ teaspoon pure vanilla extract

FOR THE COFFEE CAKE

Adjust an oven rack to the middle position and preheat the oven to 350°F [180°C]. Grease a 9 by 13 in [23 by 33 cm] pan and line it with a parchment sling (see page 16).

continued

In a medium bowl or liquid measuring cup, whisk together the milk, egg whites, crème fraîche, and vanilla. • In the bowl of a stand mixer fitted with a paddle, combine the flour, granulated sugar, baking powder, and salt. With the mixer running on low speed, add the butter one piece at a time, beating until the mixture resembles coarse sand. With the mixer still running on low speed, slowly add a little more than half of the wet ingredients. Increase the speed to medium and beat until the ingredients are incorporated, about 30 seconds. Lower the speed to low and add the rest of the wet ingredients, mixing until just combined. Increase the speed to medium and beat for 20 seconds (the batter may still look a little bumpy). Scrape down the sides and bottom of the bowl and use a spatula to mix the batter a few more times. • Pour all but 1 tablespoon of the batter into the prepared pan and smooth the top.

FOR THE CREAM CHEESE FILLING
In a small bowl, whisk together the cream cheese, granulated sugar, and the reserved 1 tablespoon of cake batter. Dollop the cream cheese filling over the cake and use a knife or an offset spatula to swirl it into the batter. Sprinkle the streusel evenly over the top. Tap the pan gently on the counter twice to help get rid of any air bubbles. • Bake for 28 to 35 minutes, rotating the pan halfway through, until the cake is golden brown and a wooden skewer or toothpick inserted into the center comes

out with a faint bit of crumbs. Transfer the cake in the pan to a wire rack and let cool for 5 minutes.

FOR THE ICING

While the cake is baking, in a medium bowl, whisk together the confectioners' sugar, 2 tablespoons of the water, the melted butter, and vanilla until smooth. Add more water, 1 tablespoon at a time, to thin the icing to your preferred consistency. • Pour half of the icing over the warm cake and let sit for 20 minutes, then pour the remaining icing over the cake and let sit while the cake finishes cooling. • Remove the cake from the pan using the parchment sling. Cut into pieces and serve. Alternatively, the cake can be left in the pan and covered in plastic wrap, then stored in the refrigerator for 2 days.

NOTE

Because the egg whites aren't being whipped for volume, store-bought egg whites will work here; just make sure they are 100 percent liquid egg whites.

VARIATION

Lemon Streusel Coffee Cake

Omit the cream cheese filling and instead dollop ¾ cup [240 g] Lemon Curd (page 208) over the cake before adding the streusel. Replace the water in the icing with fresh lemon juice.

Panettone Scones

"A big jug of coffee had just been set in the hearth, the seed-cakes were gone, and the dwarves were starting on a round of buttered scones, when there came—a loud knock."
—J. R. R. Tolkien, *The Hobbit*

I make scones for every possible occasion, and I especially love them around the holidays, as they can be shaped ahead of time and frozen, then pulled out and baked as needed. And while knocks at the door typically don't result in dragon adventures like Bilbo's above, I have found them to result in very happy guests when warm scones emerge from the oven.

⅓ cup [65 g] granulated sugar, plus more for sprinkling

1 tablespoon orange zest

2¼ cups [320 g] all-purpose flour, plus more as needed

1 tablespoon baking powder

½ teaspoon salt

½ cup [120 g] Crème Fraîche (page 205) or sour cream

¼ cup [60 g] heavy cream, plus more for brushing

1 large egg plus 1 large egg yolk

1 teaspoon pure vanilla extract

12 tablespoons [1½ sticks or 170 g] unsalted butter, cut into ½ in [12 mm] pieces

½ cup [70 g] dried fruit (cherries, apricots, Candied Orange Peels [page 201], candied ginger, cranberries, or pineapple are all good options)

8 oz [226 g] almond paste

Adjust an oven rack to the middle position and preheat the oven to 400°F [200°C]. Stack two sheet pans on top of each other and line the top sheet with parchment paper. • In a large bowl, use your hands to combine the sugar and orange zest, rubbing the orange into the sugar. Add the flour, baking powder, and salt and whisk to combine. • In a medium bowl or liquid measuring cup, whisk together the crème fraîche, heavy cream, egg, egg yolk, and vanilla.

continued

Add the butter to the dry ingredients and use a pastry cutter to cut in the butter until the flour-coated pieces are the size of peas. Add the wet ingredients and fold with a spatula until just combined. Add the dried fruit, gently folding it into the dough. • Transfer the dough to a lightly floured surface and knead four to six times, until it comes together, adding flour as necessary, as the dough will be sticky. Pat the dough gently into a square and roll it into a 12 in [30.5 cm] square (again, dusting with flour as necessary). Fold the dough in thirds, similar to a business letter. Fold the short ends of the dough in thirds again, making a square. Transfer it to a floured sheet pan or plate and place it in the freezer for 10 minutes. • While the dough is chilling, roll the almond paste into a square, roughly 12 in [30.5 cm]. • Return the dough to the floured surface, roll it into a 12 in [30.5 cm] square, and place the rolled almond paste on top. Fold the dough in thirds. Place the dough seam-side down and gently roll the dough into a 12 by 4 in [30.5 by 10 cm] rectangle.

With a sharp knife, cut it crosswise into four equal rectangles, then cut each rectangle diagonally into two triangles. Transfer the triangles to the prepared sheet pan. • Brush the tops of the triangles with a little heavy cream, making sure it doesn't drip down the sides, and sprinkle the tops generously with sugar. Bake for 18 to 25 minutes, rotating the pan halfway through, until the tops and bottoms are light golden brown. Transfer the sheet pan to a wire rack and let the scones cool for 10 minutes before serving. Scones are best eaten the same day they are made.

NOTES

Scones can be cut into circles with a biscuit cutter, instead of making triangles. I stack two sheet pans when baking the scones to keep the bottoms from browning too quickly.

Panettone Scones

TO FREEZE SCONES

Once the unbaked scones are cut into triangles, freeze them in a single layer on a sheet pan. When the scones are frozen solid, transfer them to a freezer-safe bag. They will keep in the freezer for 2 weeks. Bake as directed, adding a few minutes to the bake time.

Cheater's Croissant Dough

This dough is inspired by many different recipes, but specifically Dominique Ansel's croissant MasterClass and Mandy Lee's laminated dough in her book *The Art of Escapism Cooking*. Mandy skips using the butter in a block, instead spreading room-temperature butter over the surface of the dough, and then proceeds with folds. The results are still amazingly flaky, and it works great in applications such as Morning Buns (page 40), Cranberries and Cream Danish (page 47), and Cruffins (page 174).

1½ cups [360 g] warm water (100°F to 110°F [35°C to 45°C])	4 cups plus 1 tablespoon [577 g] all-purpose flour, plus more for dusting	¼ cup plus 1 tablespoon [63 g] granulated sugar	1½ cups [3 sticks or 339 g] unsalted European butter (preferably 83 to 84 percent butterfat), at room temperature (68°F [20°C]) and pliable
4 teaspoons active dry yeast		2 teaspoons salt	
		2 tablespoons unsalted butter, melted	

Grease a large bowl and set aside. In a small bowl or liquid measuring cup, stir together the water and yeast and let sit until dissolved, about 5 minutes. • In the bowl of a stand mixer fitted with the hook, mix together 4 cups [568 g] of the flour, the sugar, and salt. Start the mixer on low speed and add the water-yeast mixture, followed by the melted butter.

Continue to mix until all the ingredients are combined, 3 or 4 minutes (see notes, facing page). The dough will be rough and bumpy but should be in one piece. Move the dough to the large greased bowl and cover with plastic wrap. Let the dough rise at room temperature for 1½ to 2 hours, until doubled in size. • Gently press down on the dough, releasing as much gas as possible. Place the dough on a large piece of plastic wrap and shape it into a 10 by 12 in [25 by 30.5 cm] rectangle. Cover the dough with more plastic wrap, place it on a sheet pan, and transfer it to the refrigerator for at least 2 hours and up to overnight. • In the bowl of a stand mixer fitted with a paddle, beat the European butter and the remaining 1 tablespoon of flour together until creamy and combined, 2 to 3 minutes (see notes). • Remove the dough from the refrigerator, unwrap it from the plastic, and place it on a lightly floured work surface. Roll the dough into a 12 by 20 in [30.5 by 50 cm] rectangle. Spread the entire rectangle evenly with the butter-flour mixture, leaving a ½ in [12 mm] border around the rectangle. Make the first turn, or letter fold: Starting with a short side facing you, fold one-third of the dough onto itself, making sure the edges are lined up with each other. Then fold the remaining one-third of dough on top of the side that has already been folded. Rotate the dough so the seam is facing to the right and one open end is facing you. Gently roll the dough into a 10 by 18 in [25 by 46 cm] rectangle. (Each time you roll, the rectangle will get a bit smaller. *See how-to photos, pages 72–73.*) Repeat the letter fold. Sprinkle flour on a sheet pan or plate, place the dough on it, and freeze the dough for 6 minutes—set a timer so you don't forget (see notes; this helps cool the dough slightly and makes the last turn less messy). Remove the dough from the freezer and repeat the letter fold again, making sure the seam is facing to the right. Roll the dough again into a rectangle, about 8 by 16 in [20 by 40.5 cm]. Repeat the steps for one letter fold. Gently compress the dough with the rolling pin and, depending on the recipe you are using, keep the dough in one piece or cut the dough into two equal portions. If using the dough immediately, place the piece being used in the freezer for 6 minutes to chill, then proceed with the recipe. Otherwise, wrap the dough in plastic wrap, place it in a freezer-safe bag, and freeze for up to 2 weeks. The dough can be removed from the freezer the night before using and placed in the refrigerator to thaw.

NOTES

Don't overmix the dough when combining ingredients; this can result in a tough, chewy texture. • Make sure the European butter and flour mixture is pliable but not melting; it should have the texture of cream cheese and should spread easily. • Don't forget to remove the dough from the freezer after 6 minutes! If left in longer, the butter will start to freeze and then break apart as it rolls out. If you forget about the dough in the freezer, let it sit at room temperature for a while until it can be rolled out easily. The laminating process will help strengthen your dough.

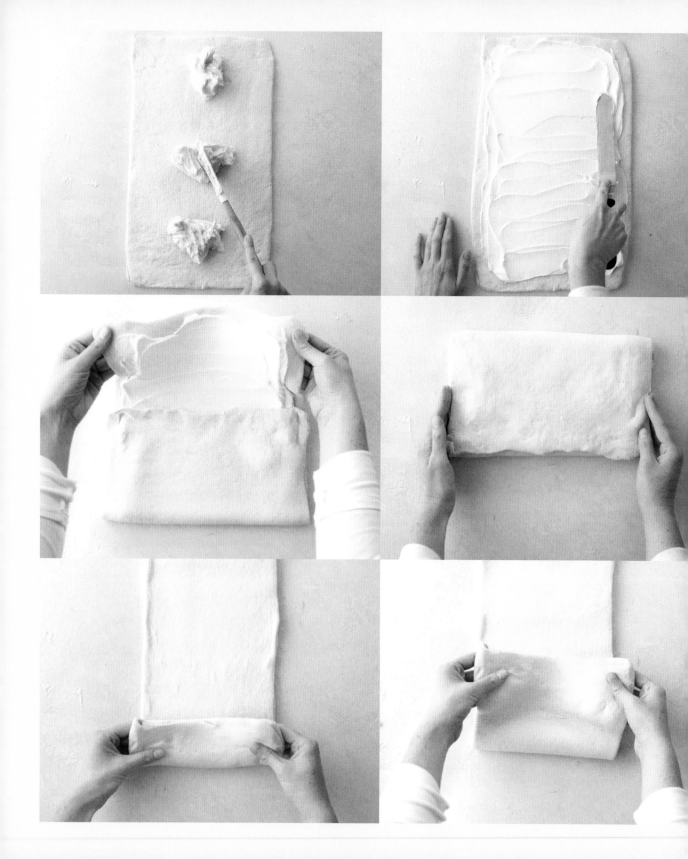

Easy Danish Dough

This dough bakes up softer and less flaky than the Cheater's Croissant Dough (page 70) but is just as easy to make. Traditional Danish dough is often flavored with cardamom, and I recommend adding it here.

¾ cup [180 g] warm whole milk (100°F to 110°F [35°F to 45°C])

1 large egg plus 2 large egg yolks, at room temperature

1 teaspoon pure vanilla extract

2½ cups [355 g] all-purpose flour, plus more for dusting

2 tablespoons granulated sugar

2¼ teaspoons instant yeast

1 teaspoon salt

1 teaspoon ground cardamom (optional)

4 tablespoons [57 g] unsalted butter, at room temperature

12 tablespoons [1½ sticks or 170 g] unsalted butter, cold, cut into 24 pieces, plus more for greasing the bowl

Grease a large bowl and set aside. In a large liquid measuring cup, combine the milk, egg, yolks, and vanilla. • In the bowl of a stand mixer fitted with a paddle, mix the flour, sugar, yeast, salt, and cardamom, if using, on low speed. Add the room-temperature butter and mix on low speed until it is incorporated into the flour and no pieces are visible. Add the cold butter and mix on low speed until it is broken down and smashed a bit but still in ½ in [12 mm] pieces. Add the milk mixture and mix on low speed until combined. The dough will be very sticky and there will be visible lumps of butter. Using a spatula, scrape the dough into the prepared bowl, cover tightly with plastic wrap, and refrigerate overnight or for up to 3 days. • The next morning, transfer the dough to a well-floured work surface. Knead ten to twelve times until the dough forms a ball. Lightly dust the top with flour and cover with a tea towel; let

rest until it comes to room temperature. Pat the dough into a 6 in [15 cm] square and roll into a 16 by 20 in [40.5 by 50 cm] rectangle. If the dough sticks at all, sprinkle more flour underneath it. Brush any excess flour off the dough and, using a bench scraper, fold the short ends of the dough over the middle to make three layers, similar to a business letter. This is the first turn. (Each time you roll, the rectangle will get a bit smaller. *See how-to photos, pages 72–73*.) • Flip the dough over (seam-side down) and roll into an 8 by 16 in [20 by 40.5 cm] rectangle. Fold the short ends over the middle

again. Repeat the steps for a total of four turns. • On the last turn, gently use the rolling pin to compress the layers together slightly. Wrap the dough tightly in plastic wrap and chill for at least 1 hour before using, or keep refrigerated for up to 2 days.

Sweet Dough

This dough is almost no-knead; it is gently folded over itself a few times during the rise time (this helps improve the dough's structure, ensures gluten will form, and makes it easier to handle). It is enriched with butter and milk, and bakes up fluffy and delicious.

4 large eggs, at room temperature

¾ cup [180 g] warm whole milk (100°F to 110°F [35°C to 45°C])

¼ cup [85 g] honey

4 cups [568 g] all-purpose flour

2¼ teaspoons instant yeast (see notes)

2 teaspoons salt

10 tablespoons [1¼ sticks or 142 g] unsalted butter, at room temperature, cut into 1 in [2.5 cm] pieces, plus more for greasing the bowl

Grease a large bowl and set aside. In a large liquid measuring cup, combine the eggs, milk, and honey. • In the bowl of a stand mixer fitted with a paddle, mix together the flour, yeast, and salt on low speed. Add the egg mixture and mix on low speed to combine. With the mixer still running on low speed, add the butter one piece at a time, then increase the speed to medium and beat until all the butter is incorporated, 1 minute. Scrape the dough into the prepared bowl; it will be very sticky. • Cover the bowl with plastic wrap and let rise for 30 minutes. Place your fingers under the dough and gently pull it up and over itself. Turn the bowl slightly and repeat. Repeat six to eight more times. Re-cover the bowl with plastic wrap and let

rise for 30 minutes. Repeat this series of folding three more times, for a rise time of 2 hours and a total of four foldings. Tightly cover the bowl with plastic wrap and refrigerate overnight or for up to 72 hours.

NOTES

If you don't chill the dough after folding, it will be hard to roll out because it will be sticky. • If you don't have instant yeast, you can use active yeast. It has larger granules, so dissolve it in the warm milk instead of adding it to the flour mixture.

2

"The children were nestled all snug in their beds, while visions of sugarplums danced in their heads."

Holiday Desserts

White Cake

with Cranberries and White Chocolate Buttercream

This is my favorite white cake (and also the base in Streusel Coffee Cake, page 63), and while I'd eat it perfectly plain, adding cranberry jam, white chocolate buttercream, and sugared cranberries is not a bad idea, either. Store-bought cranberry jam can be used if you're looking to streamline this recipe a bit.

CAKE

1 cup [240 g] whole milk, at room temperature

1 scant cup [210 g] large egg whites (from 6 or 7 large eggs), at room temperature (see note, page 83)

½ cup [120 g] Crème Fraîche (page 205) or sour cream, at room temperature

1 tablespoon pure vanilla extract

2¾ cups [391 g] all-purpose flour

2 cups [400 g] granulated sugar

4 teaspoons baking powder

1 teaspoon salt

1 cup [2 sticks or 227 g] unsalted butter, at room temperature, cut into 1 in [2.5 cm] pieces

WHITE CHOCOLATE BUTTERCREAM

8 oz [226 g] good white chocolate, chopped

1½ cups [3 sticks or 339 g] unsalted butter, at room temperature

3 tablespoons light corn syrup

Pinch salt

2 cups [240 g] confectioners' sugar

2 tablespoons heavy cream

1 tablespoon pure vanilla extract

SUGARED CRANBERRIES

¾ cup [180 g] water

1¼ cups [250 g] granulated sugar

Pinch salt

1 teaspoon pure vanilla extract

6 oz [170 g] fresh cranberries

ASSEMBLY

Cranberry Jam (page 202)

continued

FOR THE CAKE

Adjust an oven rack to the middle position and preheat the oven to 350°F [180°C]. Butter and flour three 8 by 2 in [20 by 5 cm] round cake pans and line the bottoms with parchment paper (see page 16). • In a medium bowl or liquid measuring cup, whisk together the milk, egg whites, crème fraîche, and vanilla. • In the bowl of a stand mixer fitted with a paddle, combine the flour, granulated sugar, baking powder, and salt. With the mixer running on low speed, add the butter one piece at a time, beating until the mixture resembles coarse sand. With the mixer still running on low speed, slowly add a little more than half of the wet ingredients. Increase the speed to medium and beat until the ingredients are incorporated, about 30 seconds. Return the mixer to low speed and add the rest of the wet ingredients, mixing until just combined. Increase the speed to medium and beat for 20 seconds (the batter may still look a little bumpy). Scrape down the sides and bottom of the bowl and use a spatula to mix the batter a few more times. • Divide the batter between the prepared pans and smooth the tops. Tap the pans gently on the counter two times each to help get rid of any bubbles. • Bake for 28 to 35 minutes, rotating the pans halfway through, until the cakes are golden brown and a wooden skewer or toothpick inserted into the centers comes out with a faint bit of crumbs, or a finger gently pressed into the top leaves a slight indentation. • Transfer the pans to a wire rack and let cool for 30 minutes. Turn the cakes out onto the rack, remove the parchment paper, and let cool completely. Once cool, the cakes can be frosted or wrapped in plastic wrap and refrigerated overnight or frozen for up to 1 week.

FOR THE BUTTERCREAM

Pour 1 in [2.5 cm] of water into a medium saucepan and bring it to a gentle boil over medium heat. • Melt the white chocolate in a heatproof bowl set over the pan of boiling water, being careful not to let the water touch the bottom of the bowl. Stir constantly until just melted and set aside to cool. • In the bowl of a stand mixer fitted with a paddle, beat the butter on medium speed until light yellow and creamy, about 3 minutes. Add the corn syrup and salt and mix on medium speed until combined. Lower the speed to low and gradually add the confectioners' sugar, then increase the speed to medium and beat until smooth and creamy, stopping to scrape down the sides of the bowl as necessary, 2 to 3 minutes. Add the cooled white chocolate and beat on low speed until completely combined. Add the heavy cream and vanilla and mix again on low speed until combined.

FOR THE SUGARED CRANBERRIES

Combine the water, ¾ cup [150 g] of the granulated sugar, and the salt in a medium saucepan over medium-high heat. Bring to a gentle boil and turn the heat down to medium; let simmer until the mixture is reduced slightly, 5 to 7 minutes. Pour the vanilla into the sugar liquid and stir to combine. • Pour the liquid into a medium-size container. Add the cranberries

to the sugar liquid, cover and refrigerate, and let them soak for at least 8 hours and up to 24 hours. • After the cranberries have soaked, place the remaining ½ cup [100 g] of granulated sugar in a bowl and line a sheet pan with parchment paper. Use a slotted spoon to remove some of the cranberries from the liquid and roll them in the bowl of sugar to coat. Place the coated cranberries on the sheet pan and let them dry. Repeat with the remaining cranberries. Cranberries can be stored in an airtight container in the refrigerator for up to 2 days.

TO ASSEMBLE

Place one layer of cake on a turntable or serving plate. Use an offset spatula to spread the top evenly with 3 tablespoons of the cranberry jam. Place the second layer on top and frost with another 3 tablespoons of the jam, then place the final layer on top and evenly coat the entire cake with the buttercream. The cake can be stored, covered, in the refrigerator for 24 hours. Let the cake come to room temperature and top with the cranberries just before serving.

NOTE

Because the egg whites aren't being whipped for volume, store-bought egg whites will work here; just make sure they are 100 percent liquid egg whites.

Carrot Cake
with Burnt Honey Buttercream

*"I have named you queen. / There are taller than you, taller. /
There are purer than you, purer. / There are lovelier than you, lovelier. /
But you are the queen." —Pablo Neruda*

These lines often come to mind whenever I create this cake—the pale, sweeping buttercream brings to mind piles of snow for sleigh-riding Narnian queens to glide upon, and the cinnamon-spice mixed with earthy carrots will warm you right to your toes.

CARROT CAKE

1 scant cup [210 g] large egg whites (from 6 or 7 large eggs), at room temperature

1 cup [240 g] whole milk, at room temperature

¼ cup [60 g] canola oil

2 tablespoons sour cream, at room temperature

1 teaspoon pure vanilla extract

3 cups [426 g] all-purpose flour

1 cup [200 g] granulated sugar

1 cup [200 g] light brown sugar

4 teaspoons baking powder

2 teaspoons ground cinnamon (see notes, page 87)

1 teaspoon salt

Pinch cloves

12 tablespoons [1½ sticks or 170 g] unsalted butter, at room temperature, cut into 1 in [2.5 cm] pieces

4 cups [400 g] finely grated carrots

BURNT HONEY BUTTERCREAM

1 cup plus 2 tablespoons [280 g] large eggs whites (from 7 or 8 large eggs), at room temperature

¼ teaspoon cream of tartar

1½ cups [300 g] granulated sugar

½ cup [170 g] honey

¼ teaspoon salt

¼ cup [60 g] water

3 cups [6 sticks or 678 g] unsalted butter, at room temperature, cut into 1 in [2.5 cm] pieces

1 teaspoon pure vanilla extract

ASSEMBLY

Candied Nuts (pecan variation, page 207), for decorating (optional)

continued

FOR THE CAKE

Adjust an oven rack to the middle position and preheat the oven to 350°F [180°C]. Grease three 8 by 2 in [20 by 5 cm] circular cake pans and line the bottoms with parchment paper (see page 16). • In a medium bowl or liquid measuring cup, whisk together the egg whites, milk, oil, sour cream, and vanilla. • In the bowl of a stand mixer fitted with a paddle, whisk together the flour, granulated and brown sugars, baking powder, cinnamon, salt, and cloves by hand until combined. With the mixer running on low speed, add the butter one piece at a time, beating until the mixture resembles coarse sand. With the mixer still running on low speed, slowly add a little more than half of the wet ingredients. Increase the speed to medium and beat until the ingredients are incorporated, about 30 seconds. With the mixer running on low speed, add the rest of the wet ingredients, mixing until just combined. Increase the speed to medium and beat for 20 seconds (the batter may still look a little bumpy). Scrape down the sides and bottom of the bowl, add the grated carrots, and use a spatula to mix the batter until the carrots are incorporated. • Pour the batter into the prepared pans and smooth the tops. Tap the pans gently on the counter a few times to get rid of any bubbles. Bake for 30 to 36 minutes, rotating the pans halfway through, until the cakes are golden brown and a wooden skewer or toothpick inserted into the center comes out with a faint bit of crumbs. Transfer the pans to a wire rack and let cool for 30 minutes. Turn the cakes out onto the rack, remove the parchment paper, and let cool completely.

FOR THE BUTTERCREAM

In the bowl of a stand mixer fitted with a whisk, beat the egg whites and cream of tartar on medium speed until they are almost able to hold soft peaks, 5 to 7 minutes. Lower the speed to low and add ½ cup [100 g] of the granulated sugar in a slow, steady stream. Beat on medium speed until the whites are stiff and glossy, 1 to 2 minutes. Let the whites sit in the bowl while you make the syrup. • Place the remaining 1 cup [200 g] of granulated sugar, the honey, and salt in a medium saucepan. • Pour the water over the top and gently stir just enough to wet the sugar, being careful not to mix too much so the sugar doesn't splash up the sides of the pan. Heat over medium heat, giving the pan a little shake every once in a while, to mix the honey and sugar as they melt. When the sugar has melted and the liquid looks clear (no sugar granulates are noticeable), increase the heat to medium-high and let the liquid bubble and boil until it turns a deep golden brown, 3 to 4 minutes. Remove the pan from the heat. • With the mixer running on low speed, very carefully pour about 2 tablespoons of the hot honey caramel into the egg whites, trying not to hit the sides of the bowl, and mixing until combined (pouring the hot mixture into a liquid measuring cup with a pourable spout works best here). Pour 2 tablespoons more caramel into the egg whites and continue mixing (this will help temper the eggs so they won't cook). With the mixer running on low speed, pour the rest of the caramel

into the whites in a slow, steady stream, still trying not to hit the sides of the bowl. Beat until the mixture is completely combined. • Increase the speed to medium-high and whisk until the bowl cools to room temperature. Lower the speed to low and add the butter one piece at a time, beating well after each addition. Increase the speed to medium and beat until the buttercream is completely smooth, 2 to 3 minutes. Add the vanilla and beat on medium speed for 1 to 2 minutes.

TO ASSEMBLE

Place one layer of the cake on a turntable or serving plate. With an offset spatula, spread the top evenly with 1½ cups [450 g] of the buttercream. Place the second layer on top, and frost with another 1 cup [300 g] of filling. Place the third layer on top and frost the cake, topping with the candied pecans, if desired, and serve. Store the cake, covered, in the refrigerator for up to 1 day.

NOTES

If you want more spice, add ¾ teaspoon of ginger and ¼ teaspoon of nutmeg along with the cinnamon. • This carrot cake can be made with cream cheese frosting instead of the Burnt Honey Buttercream; if that is your preference, use the frosting from the Confetti Cake (page 183) instead.

Triple Chocolate Mousse Cake

There are so many recipes for triple chocolate mousse cake, and all of them are delicious, I'm sure. This version is based on bars of the same name from my last book, *100 Cookies*. Making them in cake form means there is more chocolate mousse in every bite. I've also swapped out whipped cream on top for chocolate ganache, which makes this a chocolate lover's dream.

CRUST

1½ cups [150 g] chocolate wafer cookies

3 tablespoons unsalted butter, melted

CAKE

6 oz [170 g] semisweet or bittersweet chocolate

8 tablespoons [1 stick or 113 g] unsalted butter

2 tablespoons Dutch-process cocoa powder

1 cup [200 g] granulated sugar

4 large eggs, at room temperature

1 teaspoon pure vanilla extract

¼ teaspoon salt

¼ cup [36 g] all-purpose flour

CHOCOLATE MOUSSE

1¾ cups [420 g] heavy cream

5 large egg yolks, at room temperature

¼ cup [50 g] granulated sugar

¼ teaspoon salt

1 teaspoon pure vanilla extract

8 oz [226 g] semisweet or bittersweet chocolate, finely chopped

CHOCOLATE GANACHE

6 oz [170 g] semisweet or bittersweet chocolate

½ cup [120 g] heavy cream

Cocoa powder, for dusting

89

•

Holiday Desserts

continued

FOR THE CRUST

Adjust an oven rack to the middle position and preheat the oven to 350°F [180°C]. Grease a 9 in [23 cm] springform pan. • Place the cookies in the bowl of a food processor and process until broken down into fine crumbs. Transfer the crumbs to a medium bowl and pour the melted butter over the top. Use a spatula to stir together until combined. • Press the mixture onto the bottom of the prepared pan and bake for 10 minutes. Remove the pan from the oven and let cool while preparing the cake batter. Leave the oven on.

FOR THE CAKE

In a small saucepan over low heat, melt the chocolate and butter, stirring frequently until smooth. Remove from the heat and stir in the cocoa powder. • In a large bowl, whisk together the sugar, eggs, vanilla, and salt until smooth. Add the flour and mix again until combined. Add the warm chocolate and whisk into the batter until combined. Let the mixture sit for 15 minutes. • Pour the cake batter over the cooled crust and use an offset spatula to smooth the top. Bake until the edges are set and the center jiggles slightly, 22 to 27 minutes. Remove from the oven and let the cake cool completely on a wire rack. Once cool, cover the pan with plastic wrap and refrigerate for 4 hours, or overnight.

FOR THE CHOCOLATE MOUSSE

Heat 1 cup [240 g] of the heavy cream in a small, heavy saucepan over medium heat until just warmed. • In a medium saucepan off the heat, whisk the egg yolks. Whisking constantly, slowly add the sugar to the egg yolks, then the salt, and then slowly pour in the warmed heavy cream. Cook over medium heat, stirring constantly, until the mixture thickens, coats the back of a spoon, and registers 160°F [70°C]. Pour the mixture through a fine-mesh sieve into a large bowl and stir in the vanilla. • In a small saucepan over low heat, melt the chocolate, stirring frequently until smooth. Whisk the chocolate into the custard until smooth, then let cool. • In the bowl of a stand mixer fitted with a whisk, beat the remaining ¾ cup [180 g] of heavy cream until stiff peaks form. Whisk one-third of the whipped cream into the chocolate custard to lighten it, then gently fold in the remaining whipped cream. • Pour the chocolate mousse on top of the baked, chilled cake. Use an offset spatula to even the top. Return the cake to the refrigerator and let chill for 8 hours or up to overnight.

Place the chocolate in a small bowl. • Heat the heavy cream in a small saucepan over medium-low heat until it is simmering and just about to boil. Pour the cream over the chocolate, cover the bowl with plastic wrap, and let sit for 5 minutes. Remove the plastic wrap and use a butter knife to stir the chocolate into the cream until it is completely smooth. Let the mixture cool to almost room temperature. Once cool and ready to use, stir the ganache a few times before using.

Pour the chocolate ganache over the top of the cake, right in the center. Using an offset spatula, cover the whole top with the ganache, carefully smoothing it out as you move it to the edges. Let the ganache set before slicing. Unmold the cake from the springform pan, dust with cocoa powder, if desired, and serve. Cake can be stored, covered, in the refrigerator for 24 hours.

VARIATION

Triple Chocolate Mint Mousse Cake

Add 1 teaspoon of mint extract to the cake base along with the vanilla.
Cover the top of the cake with crushed candy cane pieces right before serving.

91

Hazelnut Cheesecake

Half of my family is a cheesecake kind of family, and the other half will take pie, thank you. When I'm making dessert for special occasions, I always try to include at least one cheesecake—the creamy, rich filling is definitely a holiday indulgence. This cheesecake has a chocolate-cacao crust, a creamy hazelnut filling, and more chocolate in the form of ganache on top.

CRUST

2 cups [200 g] chocolate wafer cookies

¼ cup [30 g] cacao nibs

4 tablespoons [57 g] unsalted butter, plus more for greasing the pan

CHEESECAKE

2 lb [908 g] cream cheese, at room temperature

1½ cups [300 g] granulated sugar

½ teaspoon salt

1 cup [240 g] sour cream, at room temperature

½ cup [120 g] Frangelico

2 tablespoons unsalted butter, melted and cooled to room temperature

1 tablespoon pure vanilla extract

3 large eggs plus 1 egg yolk, at room temperature

¾ cup [180 g] heavy cream, at room temperature

GANACHE

6 oz [170 g] semisweet or bittersweet chocolate, finely chopped

¾ cup [180 g] heavy cream

ASSEMBLY

Candied Nuts (hazelnut variation, page 207), for topping (optional)

FOR THE CRUST

Adjust an oven rack to the middle position and preheat the oven to 325°F [165°C]. Grease a 9 in [23 cm] springform pan. • Place the cookies and cacao nibs in the bowl of a food processor and process until the cookies are broken down into fine crumbs. Transfer the crumbs to a medium bowl.

continued

93

Pour the melted butter over the top and use a spatula to stir together until combined. • Press the mixture onto the bottom of the prepared pan and bake for 10 minutes. Remove the pan from the oven and let cool. After the pan has cooled, wrap the outer sides in two layers of aluminum foil, with the shiny side facing out (this helps keep the sides of the cheesecake from browning).

FOR THE CHEESECAKE

In the bowl of a stand mixer fitted with a paddle, beat the cream cheese on medium speed until light and completely smooth, 4 to 5 minutes. Scrape down the sides of the bowl often, making sure all the cream cheese is silky smooth. Add the sugar and salt and beat on medium speed until completely incorporated, stopping to scrape down the sides of the bowl as needed, 2 to 3 minutes. Add the sour cream, Frangelico, butter, and vanilla and beat on medium speed for 2 to 3 minutes. Add the eggs one at a time, and then the yolk, beating on low speed after each addition until just combined. Add the heavy cream and mix on low speed until combined. Using a spatula, give the filling a couple of turns to make sure it is completely combined. • Pour the filling over the cooled crust and use an offset spatula to smooth the top. Bang the bottom of the pan on the counter a few times to help get rid of any air bubbles. • Set a large roasting pan on the floor of the oven and fill it with 4 qt [3.8 L] of boiling water (see notes, page 95). Place the springform pan on the oven rack and bake the cheesecake for 1 hour without opening the door. Check the cheesecake after 1 hour; the outer ring (2 to 3 in [5 to 7.5 cm]) of the cheesecake should be slightly puffed and fairly firm, and

the center should be set but still a bit jiggly when wiggled gently, resembling Jell-O. If the outer ring is not firm, let the cheesecake bake another 10 to 15 minutes. The center of the cheesecake should register 150°F [65°C]. Turn off the heat, open the oven door just a crack, and let the cheesecake rest and cool in the warm, humid oven for 30 minutes. • Transfer the pan to a wire rack and let cool for 5 to 10 minutes. Remove the foil from the pan and carefully run a thin knife or an offset spatula around the cake to help loosen it from the pan (this will help prevent cracking as it cools). Once the cake is completely cool, place a piece of parchment paper over the top of the pan (to keep condensation off the top of the cheesecake) and transfer to the refrigerator. Let chill for at least 6 hours or overnight.

FOR THE GANACHE

Place the chocolate in a small bowl. Heat the heavy cream in a small saucepan over medium-low heat until it is simmering and just about to boil. Pour the cream over the chocolate, cover the bowl with plastic wrap, and let sit for 5 minutes. Remove the plastic wrap and use a butter knife to stir the chocolate into the cream until it is completely smooth. Let the mixture cool to almost room temperature. Once cool and ready to use, stir the ganache a few times before using.

TO ASSEMBLE

To remove the cheesecake from the pan, run a thin, offset spatula between the sides of the cake and the pan and then gently remove the sides. Slide the spatula between the bottom of the crust and the pan to loosen it and then carefully slide the cheesecake onto a serving

plate. Pour the ganache over the top of the cheesecake, carefully smoothing it out as you move it to the edges. Sprinkle with the candied nuts, if desired. Let the ganache set before slicing. Let the cheesecake come to room temperature before serving. Cheesecake can be stored in an airtight container in the refrigerator for 1 day.

NOTES

I've always used a roasting pan of water on the floor of the oven instead of immersing the cheesecake in a water bath. The steam from the water helps prevent the cheesecake from drying and cracking. Many people argue that a water bath helps create a creamier cheesecake, but I haven't noticed a significant difference, and find this method less worrisome than trying to stick a springform in water and then moving it to the oven. • The baking time on the cheesecake is relative, and it may take longer to bake than suggested. Making sure your ingredients are room temperature, adding boiling water to the roasting pan, and using an oven thermometer to make sure your oven temperature is correct will ensure good results. Don't be afraid to bake your cheesecake longer than noted if it hasn't set; this will not hurt the cake.

Apple, Caramel, and Hard Cider Pie

Apple pie is quintessential holiday fare, and my family would be highly disappointed if it was missing from our dessert table. I have taken my favorite apple pie recipe (found in my first book) and added hard cider and caramel to it, elevating it to superstar level. The method I use for making pie comes from Ms. Rose Levy Beranbaum and her wonderful book *The Pie and Pastry Bible*. Releasing the fruit juice and then cooking it down helps control how much liquid is in the filling and gives it a more concentrated flavor.

2½ lb [1.1 kg] Gala apples, peeled, cored, and sliced into ¼ in [6 mm] pieces (7 to 8 apples)

¼ cup [50 g] light brown sugar

1 teaspoon fresh lemon juice

¼ teaspoon salt

2 tablespoons cornstarch

½ teaspoon ground cinnamon

½ cup [120 g] hard cider or apple cider

¾ cup [162 g] Caramel or Salted Caramel (page 195), at room temperature

All-purpose flour, for dusting

1 recipe Double Pie Dough (page 112)

Egg wash (see page 16)

1 to 2 tablespoons granulated sugar

No-Churn Ice Cream (page 196) or Whipped Cream (page 204), for serving

In a large bowl, combine the apples, brown sugar, lemon juice, and salt. Let sit at room temperature for 1 to 2 hours, or covered in the refrigerator overnight. Strain the sugary juice (you should have about ½ cup [120 g]) from the fruit into a medium saucepan and return the apples to the large bowl. Add the cornstarch and cinnamon to the apples and toss to combine.

continued

Add the hard cider to the saucepan with the juice and bring to a boil over medium heat. Turn the heat down to low and simmer until reduced to a scant ½ cup [120 g], 5 to 6 minutes. Remove from the heat and whisk in the caramel. • Pour the caramel mixture over the apples and toss to combine. Set aside while rolling out the pie dough. • Lightly flour a work surface and roll one piece of the dough into a 12 in [30.5 cm] circle about ¼ in [6 mm] thick and place it into a 9 in [23 cm] pie plate. Transfer the plate to the refrigerator and let the dough chill while you roll out the second piece. Lightly flour the work surface again and roll the second piece of dough into a 12 in [30.5 cm] circle, about ¼ in [6 mm] thick. • Fill the prepared pie shell with the apple mixture and place the second crust on top. Trim the dough overhang to 1 in [2.5 cm] past the lip of the pie plate. Pinch the dough together and tuck it under itself so it's resting on the edge of the pie plate. Crimp the edges of the dough and cut at least four vents in the center, each about 2 in [5 cm] long. Transfer the pie plate to the freezer to chill for about 20 minutes while the oven is preheating. The crust should be nice and firm before you bake it. • Adjust an oven rack to the lowest position and preheat the oven to 425°F [220°C]. Place a sheet pan on the oven rack (the preheated sheet pan helps crisp the bottom of the pie crust and also catches any leaks and drips). • When ready to bake, brush the top of the pie with the egg wash and sprinkle with the granulated sugar. Transfer the pie plate to the preheated sheet pan and bake for 25 minutes. Turn the heat down to 375°F [190°C] and bake for 40 to 50 minutes, until the crust is deep golden brown and the juices bubble. • Transfer the pie plate to a wire rack and let cool for at least 4 hours before serving. Serve with ice cream or whipped cream. The pie is best eaten the same day it's made.

Crème Brûlée Pumpkin Pie

This is almost straight-up pumpkin pie; as much as I like this famous dessert, I find a little crunch is essential, so I like to serve mine brûléed. While my children look terrified at the thought of anything other than whipped cream topping their slices, I find most guests enjoy the added layer. But, not to worry! If you just want your pie the old-fashioned way, you can omit the crème brûlée topping and serve with whipped cream. For more tang in your filling, you can substitute crème fraîche for part or all of the whole milk.

PUMPKIN FILLING

3 tablespoons [45 g] unsalted butter

One 15 oz [425 g] can unsweetened pumpkin purée

2 tablespoons light brown sugar

¾ teaspoon salt

1 teaspoon ground cinnamon

¾ teaspoon ground ginger

½ teaspoon nutmeg

Pinch cloves

1 tablespoon blackstrap rum (optional)

1 teaspoon vanilla extract

One 14 oz [396 g] can sweetened condensed milk

2 large eggs plus 2 large egg yolks, at room temperature

½ cup [120 g] heavy cream

½ teaspoon lemon juice (optional)

ASSEMBLY

1 Single Pie Dough (page 112), fully baked and still warm

2 to 3 tablespoons granulated sugar

Whipped Cream (page 204, optional), for serving

FOR THE PUMPKIN FILLING

Adjust an oven rack to the middle position and preheat the oven to 400°F [200°C]. •

In a large heavy-bottom saucepan over medium heat, brown the butter until golden.

continued

99

•

Holiday Desserts

Off the heat, add the pumpkin purée, brown sugar, salt, cinnamon, ginger, nutmeg, and cloves. Put the pan back over medium heat and bring the mixture to a sputtering simmer; this will take 5 to 7 minutes. Continue to simmer, stirring occasionally, until the mixture is thick and shiny, 10 to 15 minutes total. • Remove the pan from the heat and stir in the black-strap rum, if using, and the vanilla. Pour in the sweetened condensed milk, mixing until smooth and combined. Add the eggs, yolks, and heavy cream and whisk until fully incorporated. Strain the mixture through a fine-mesh sieve set over a medium bowl, using a spatula to press the solids through the sieve. Re-whisk the liquid and taste the filling. If the flavor seems dull, add ¼ teaspoon of lemon juice and whisk to combine. Taste again, adding more lemon juice, if needed (just a tiny bit at a time), until the desired flavor is reached. Transfer the filling to the warm, partially baked pie shell. • Set the pie plate on a sheet pan and transfer it to the oven to bake for 10 minutes. Turn down the heat to 300°F [150°C] and continue baking until the edges of the pie are puffed and the center jiggles slightly if shaken, 40 to 50 minutes longer.

TO ASSEMBLE

Transfer the pie to a wire rack and cool to room temperature, 4 to 6 hours (it can also be refrigerated for several hours before serving). • Just before serving, sprinkle a generous amount of granulated sugar over the entire surface of the pie. Use a kitchen torch to brûlée the top until the sugar is melted and has turned dark brown (you can also slice the pie and then torch the top, for less messy slicing). Serve the pie immediately with whipped cream, if desired.

101

Chocolate Mint Ice Cream Pie

Every Christmas Eve of my childhood was spent at my grandma's cozy little house. My family would arrive after dark to tables heaped with food and presents packed under the tree, and my tiny mind would explode taking it all in. At some point in the evening my grandma would, without fail, pull out a box of minty green ice cream Christmas trees dotted with sprinkles from the freezer and hand each grandchild one when the parents were lost in happy banter and red wine. This is a slightly classier version of that mint-filled treat but will still awaken your inner child. The crust and ice cream base can be put together a day or two in advance, which comes in handy during holiday preparations, and the meringue can be replaced with Whipped Cream (page 204).

CRUST

2 cups [200 g] chocolate wafer cookies

4 tablespoons [57 g] unsalted butter, melted

MINT NO-CHURN ICE CREAM

One 14 oz [397 g] can sweetened condensed milk

1 tablespoon pure vanilla extract

1 teaspoon mint extract (or more or less to taste)

¼ teaspoon salt

2 oz [57 g] cream cheese, at room temperature

2 cups [240 g] heavy cream

Green food coloring (optional)

MERINGUE

1 cup [200 g] granulated sugar

¾ cup [175 g] large egg whites (from 4 or 5 eggs), at room temperature

¼ teaspoon salt

¼ teaspoon cream of tartar

2 teaspoons pure vanilla extract

103

continued

FOR THE CRUST

Adjust an oven rack to the middle position and preheat the oven to 350°F [180°C]. • Place the cookies in the bowl of a food processor and process until broken down into fine crumbs. Move the crumbs to a medium bowl and pour the melted butter over the top. Use a spatula to stir together until combined. Press the mixture into the bottom and up the sides of a deep (at least 2 in [5 cm]) 9½ or 10 in [24 or 25 cm] pie plate and bake for 8 minutes. Remove the pan from the oven and let cool completely.

FOR THE ICE CREAM

In a large bowl, whisk together the condensed milk, vanilla, mint, and salt until completely combined. • In the bowl of a stand mixer fitted with a whisk, beat the cream cheese on medium speed until smooth. Lower the speed to low and add the heavy cream in a slow, steady stream, mixing until combined. Increase the speed to medium-high and whisk until stiff peaks form, 3 to 4 minutes. • Add half of the whipped cream mixture to the sweetened condensed milk mixture and whisk by hand until completely combined. Using a rubber spatula, gently fold in the remaining whipped cream mixture until no streaks remain. Add the food coloring, if using, stirring to combine. Pour the filling into the prepared pie crust and freeze until firm, 6 hours, or covered, up to 4 days.

Pour 1 in [2.5 cm] of water into a medium saucepan and bring it to a gentle boil over medium heat. • In the bowl of a stand mixer, stir the granulated sugar, egg whites, salt, and cream of tartar with a rubber spatula to combine. Place the bowl over the saucepan, being careful not to let the water touch the bottom of the bowl. Stir with the spatula until the sugar is completely melted and reaches a temperature of 160°F [70°C], 4 to 5 minutes. As you stir the mixture, scrape down the sides of the bowl with a spatula (this will ensure no sugar crystals are lurking on the sides of the bowl and will help prevent the egg whites from cooking). • Remove the bowl from the heat and place it in the stand mixer fitted with a whisk.

Whisk on low speed for 1 minute, then slowly increase the speed to medium-high. Beat until stiff, glossy, peaks form, 8 to 10 minutes. The bowl should feel cool to the touch at this point. Add the vanilla and mix on medium-low speed until incorporated. Use immediately.

TO ASSEMBLE

Take the chilled ice cream pie from the freezer. Working quickly, use a spatula to spread the meringue over the top of the pie. Use a spoon to create curls and peaks in the meringue, if desired. The pie can be served immediately or held in the freezer with the meringue topping for 8 hours.

NOTE

I like the meringue un-toasted here, but you can take a kitchen torch to it if you'd like. Remember that you are working with ice cream, so work quickly if doing so.

VARIATION

Candy Cane Cake

Add ½ cup [100 g] crushed candy canes to the sweetened condensed milk mixture. Use pink food coloring instead of green, and top the meringue with more crushed candies.

105

Bittersweet Chocolate Tart
with Irish Cream

Whenever I made this tart at the coffeehouse I worked at, it always sold out quickly. While it's delicious (which is the most important thing), I really love it because it is so easy to make. The shortbread crust is a pat-in-the-pan affair, and the filling is as easy as heating up cream and whisking things together. If you aren't a fan of Irish cream, it can be omitted.

CHOCOLATE FILLING

9 oz [255 g] bittersweet or semisweet chocolate

¾ cup [180 g] heavy cream

⅓ cup [80 g] Irish cream (optional)

1 large egg plus 2 large egg yolks, at room temperature

1 teaspoon pure vanilla extract

¼ teaspoon salt

ASSEMBLY

Shortbread Crust (page 111), baked and cooled

Whipped Cream (page 204), for serving

Adjust an oven rack to the middle position and preheat the oven to 350°F [180°C].

FOR THE FILLING

Place the chocolate in a medium bowl. Heat the heavy cream in a small saucepan over medium heat until it is simmering and just about to boil. Pour the cream over the chocolate, cover the bowl with plastic wrap, and let it sit for 5 minutes. Remove the plastic and whisk until smooth. Whisk in the Irish cream, if using, egg, egg yolks, vanilla, and salt.

TO ASSEMBLE

Pour the chocolate filling into the prepared tart shell. Bake until the center seems set but still jiggles slightly, like Jell-O, when the pan is shaken, 15 to 18 minutes. Move the pan to a wire rack to cool. Serve at room temperature with whipped cream. The tart is best eaten the day it is baked, but can be stored loosely covered in the refrigerator for up to 2 days.

Frozen Bonbons

While my grandma often had minty ice cream trees stashed in her freezer for us kids, there were also peppermint bonbons for the adults. I remember finally being offered a bonbon around age fourteen and reveling in each and every bite. Depending on what flavor of ice cream you choose, feel free to top your bonbon with something to signify what's inside: flaky sea salt for caramel, crushed chocolate-covered espresso beans for coffee, or crushed candy canes for mint. Store-bought ice cream will also work if you don't have time to make your own.

1 recipe
No-Churn Ice Cream
(page 196), flavor
of your choice,
not yet frozen

12 oz [340 g]
semisweet or
bittersweet
chocolate

Fill silicone semicircle molds with the unfrozen ice cream mixture. (You can use any size molds you want, but note that 1 tablespoon molds will give you bite-size bonbons, and using larger molds may require more melted chocolate.) Freeze the molds until the ice cream is firm, 6 hours or overnight. If you don't have molds, you can use a small cookie scoop to scoop tablespoon-size balls of frozen ice cream, place them on a sheet pan, and freeze until very firm. • When ready to assemble, line a sheet pan with parchment paper. Remove the ice cream balls from the molds, place them on the prepared sheet pan, and transfer the pan to the freezer to let the ice cream re-firm while you melt the chocolate. • In a small saucepan over low heat, melt the chocolate, stirring frequently until smooth. Pour the melted chocolate into a medium-size bowl and let cool for 10 minutes. • Working very quickly, remove one ice cream ball from the freezer and place it in the chocolate. Using a wooden skewer or fork poked into the ice cream, coat the ball in the chocolate. Lift up the bonbon and allow the excess chocolate to drip into the bowl. Set the bonbon back on the sheet pan in the freezer, then pull out another uncoated ice cream ball and repeat until all the balls are covered in chocolate. Freeze the bonbons for 20 to 30 minutes, until firm, or for up to 1 week.

109

Shortbread Crust

This is a simple, pat-in-the-pan crust that has traveled with me over the years to various coffeehouses and bakeries.

10 tablespoons [142 g] unsalted butter, at room temperature	⅓ cup [65 g] granulated sugar ½ teaspoon salt	1 large egg plus 1 large egg yolk 1 teaspoon pure vanilla extract	2 cups [284 g] all-purpose flour Egg wash (see page 16)

In the bowl of a stand mixer fitted with a paddle, beat the butter on low speed until creamy, about 1 minute. Add the sugar and salt and beat again on low speed until creamy and combined, 2 minutes. Scrape down the sides and add the egg, egg yolk, and vanilla and beat on low speed until combined. Add the flour and mix on low speed until the dough comes together. • Press the dough into the bottom and up the sides of a 10 in [25 cm] tart pan with a removable bottom (see note, page 104). Press and smooth the dough with your hands to an even thickness. Place the pan on a sheet pan and transfer to the freezer until the dough is firm, 20 to 30 minutes. • Adjust an oven rack to the middle position and preheat the oven to 350°F [180°C]. Remove the pan from the freezer and line the pan with parchment paper, covering the edges to prevent burning. Fill the center with pie weights. • Bake for 24 to 28 minutes, until the dough is light golden brown and no longer wet. Remove the tart pan from the oven and carefully remove the pie weights and parchment paper. Brush the center of the tart with the egg wash. Return the pan to the oven and bake for 3 to 6 minutes, until deep golden brown. Transfer the pan to a wire rack and let cool completely.

NOTE

Tart pans come in many different depths; some are very shallow. You will need a pan that is 1½ to 2 in [4 to 5 cm] in height for this recipe.

111

Pie Dough

I've been making this pie dough for many years and love how flaky and rich it is. If your kitchen is especially warm, you can chill the dry ingredients for 10 minutes before proceeding with the recipe.

SINGLE

8 tablespoons [1 stick or 113 g] unsalted butter, cut into 8 pieces

1½ cups [213 g] all-purpose flour, plus more for dusting

1 tablespoon granulated sugar

½ teaspoon salt

1 cup [240 g] ice water

DOUBLE

18 tablespoons [2¼ sticks or 255 g] unsalted butter, cut into 18 pieces

2½ cups [355 g] all-purpose flour, plus more for dusting

2 tablespoons granulated sugar

1 teaspoon salt

1 cup [240 g] ice water

Place the butter pieces in a small bowl and transfer it to the freezer for 5 to 10 minutes. • In the bowl of a stand mixer fitted with a paddle, mix the flour, sugar, and salt on low speed until combined. Add half of the chilled butter and mix on low speed until the butter is just starting to break down, about 1 minute. Add the rest of the butter and continue mixing until the butter is broken down in various sizes (some butter will be incorporated into the dough, some pieces will be a bit large, but most should be about the size of small peas). Stop the mixer and use your hands to check for any dry patches of flour on the bottom of the bowl; incorporate the flour as best you can. With the mixer running on low speed, slowly add about ¼ cup [60 g] of the ice water and mix until the dough starts to come together but is still quite shaggy (if the dough is not coming together, add more water, 1 tablespoon at a time, until it does). • Transfer the dough to a lightly floured work surface and flatten it slightly into a square. Gather any loose/dry pieces that won't stick to the dough and place them on top of the square. • Gently fold the dough over onto itself and then flatten into a square again. Repeat this process three or four more times until all the loose pieces are worked into the dough, being careful not to overwork the dough. Flatten the dough one last time, form it into one 6 in [15 cm] disk (if making a single) or two 6 in [15 cm] disks (if making a double), and wrap the dough in plastic wrap. Refrigerate the dough for 30 minutes (and up to 2 days) before using.

BAKING A SINGLE CRUST
Lightly flour a work surface and roll the dough into a 12 in [30.5 cm] circle. Gently fold the dough in quarters and transfer it into a 9 in [23 cm] pie plate. Unfold the dough, letting the excess dough drape over the edges of the plate. Gently press the dough into the bottom and trim the overhang to 1 in [2.5 cm] past the lip. Tuck the overhanging dough so the folded edge lies on the edge of the plate. Crimp the edge of the dough with your fingers and place the pie plate in the freezer until the dough is firm, 20 to 30 minutes. • Adjust an oven rack to the lowest position and preheat the oven to 400°F [200°C]. Place a sheet pan on the oven rack (the preheated pan helps crisp the bottom of the pie crust). Remove the pie plate from the freezer and line the pie shell with parchment paper, covering the edges to prevent burning. Fill the center with pie weights and bake as directed below.

PARTIALLY BAKED CRUST:
Bake for 25 to 28 minutes, until the dough is golden brown and no longer wet. Transfer the pie plate to a wire rack and carefully remove the pie weights and parchment paper. Finish the pie as directed in the recipe.

FULLY BAKED CRUST:
Bake for 25 to 28 minutes, until the dough is golden brown and no longer wet. Transfer the pie plate to a wire rack and carefully remove the pie weights and parchment paper. Return the pie plate to the oven and continue to bake for 8 to 12 minutes, until deep golden brown. Transfer the pie plate to a wire rack and let cool completely. Finish the pie as directed in the recipe.

3

"Howling wind or falling snow aside,
the best reading companion is the
smell of something baking in the oven."

−NIGEL SLATER, *THE CHRISTMAS CHRONICLES*

Gift
Giving

Caramel Candies

Homemade caramels are the bee's knees. While I enjoy a basic caramel as much as anyone else does, I highly recommend trying the variations below: Triple sec adds a lovely orange flavor, the salted caramels are divine, and espresso will wow any coffee lover.

1¾ cups [350 g] granulated sugar

½ cup [160 g] light corn syrup

¼ cup [60 g] water

½ teaspoon salt

1¼ cups [300 g] heavy cream

6 tablespoons [85 g] unsalted butter, plus more for greasing the pan

1 tablespoon pure vanilla extract

Grease an 8 by 4 in [20 by 10 cm] loaf pan and line it with a parchment sling so that the paper comes up all the sides and has about a 2 in [5 cm] overhang on each side (see page 16). Grease the parchment paper. • In a large, heavy-bottom saucepan (the caramel will bubble up quite a bit once it starts cooking, so it's important to have a deep pan) over medium-high heat, combine the sugar, corn syrup, water, and salt, stirring very gently to combine while trying to avoid getting any sugar crystals on the sides of the pan. Cover and bring to a boil, until the sugar has melted and the mixture is clear, 3 to 5 minutes. Uncover and cook until the sugar has turned light golden and reaches 300°F [150°C] on an instant-read

thermometer, 6 to 7 minutes. Turn the heat down to medium and cook until deep golden (340°F [170°C]), about 4 to 5 minutes more. Immediately remove the pan from the heat and add the heavy cream and butter (the cream will foam considerably, so be careful pouring it in). Return the pan to medium-high heat and cook until the caramel reaches the desired stage, stirring frequently, 4 to 7 minutes. For soft, melt-in-your mouth caramels, cook until 248°F [120°C], and for firmer caramels with a bit more chew, cook until 252°F [122°C]. Stir in the vanilla off the heat. Let the caramel sit for 2 to 3 minutes, until the bubbles subside. • Carefully pour the caramel into the prepared pan and gently tap the pan on the counter a few times to eliminate any air bubbles. Let the caramel cool completely, then transfer to the refrigerator and chill for 1 hour. • Using the parchment overhang, lift the caramel out of the pan. Peel away the parchment paper and cut the caramel in half lengthwise, then cut each half into twelve 2 in [5 cm] pieces, for 24 rectangular pieces. Candies can be left as rectangles, or cut again into squares, for a total of 48 pieces. Individually wrap each caramel in wax paper or cellophane, twisting the ends of the paper closed. The wrapped caramels can be stored in an airtight container at room temperature for up to 2 weeks.

Orange Caramel

Add 1 tablespoon of triple sec and 2 teaspoons of grated orange zest to the caramels along with the vanilla.

Espresso Caramels

Add 1 teaspoon of finely ground espresso and 1 tablespoon of strong, freshly brewed coffee along with the vanilla.

Salted Caramels

Top each cut piece of caramel with a sprinkle of fleur de sel before wrapping.

Peanut Butter Cups

I don't know if the world needs another recipe for peanut butter cups, but I've been making these around the holidays for years, much to the delight of my family, and thought you may enjoy making them, too. Use silicone molds to get a nice shape and glossy chocolate.

16 oz [455 g] semisweet or bittersweet chocolate	½ cup [108 g] creamy peanut butter	2 tablespoons unsalted butter, at room temperature	Pinch salt
	¼ cup [30 g] confectioners' sugar	½ teaspoon pure vanilla extract	

In a small saucepan over low heat, melt the chocolate, stirring frequently until smooth. Pour the melted chocolate into a medium bowl and let cool for 10 minutes. • In another medium bowl, mix together the peanut butter, sugar, butter, vanilla, and salt until combined and completely smooth. • Place about a tablespoon of chocolate in the bottom of each circle in a silicone mold (you can also line a mini muffin pan and use that instead). Tilt and twist the mold around so the chocolate coats the sides of the circle. Scoop out a scant tablespoon of the peanut butter mixture and gently roll it into a ball between your palms (if it is too sticky to do so, refrigerate the mixture for 10 minutes to help it firm up). Place the ball in the center of each mold and top each one with some of the remaining chocolate. Smooth out the tops by gently tapping the mold on the counter, then chill in the refrigerator for 2 to 3 hours to set. Once set, pop each peanut butter cup out of its mold and bring to room temperature before serving. Peanut butter cups can be stored in an airtight container in the refrigerator for 1 week.

121

Gift Giving

continued

Cacao Nibs Topping

Melt 1 oz [28 g] of chocolate. Place about ½ teaspoon of chocolate on top of each set and unmolded peanut butter cup, carefully smoothing out the tops. Sprinkle with chopped cacao nibs and let set before serving.

Triple Chocolate Peppermint Bark

This recipe is inspired by and adapted from the very famous *Bon Appétit* peppermint bark recipe. I have switched it up a bit—two layers of chocolate instead of one, and slightly different chocolate ratios. I make it every year, and one batch goes a long way, especially if chopped into small triangles. For instance, you might want to give this out to friends and neighbors, or bring it to the office. And all those holiday parties you don't want to miss? What a nice little something to slip into your host's hands along with that bottle of wine.

Or you could make it with really good intentions, then set it in your fridge or your secret chocolate stash spot (try to find mine; you won't succeed) and then nibble away at it little by little when your husband is shoveling snow or your little ones are supposed to be napping. You can pretend it's a little present to yourself—a sweet chocolate gift sprinkled with peppermint and more chocolate. Merry Christmas, you.

8 oz [226 g] bittersweet chocolate, 60 to 70 percent, finely chopped

8 oz [226 g] semisweet chocolate, finely chopped

⅓ cup [80 g] heavy cream

¾ teaspoon peppermint extract

8 oz [226 g] good white chocolate, finely chopped

3 candy canes, crushed (or a handful of peppermint candies, crushed)

123

With a pencil and ruler, measure out and mark a 9 by 13 in [23 by 33 cm] rectangle on a piece of parchment paper large enough to fit in a sheet pan. Flip the paper over (so the pencil marks are on the bottom), and then place the paper on a sheet pan.

continued

Place the bittersweet chocolate in a heatproof bowl and set it over a saucepan of barely simmering water (do not allow the bottom of the bowl to touch the water). Stir occasionally until the chocolate is melted and smooth. Remove the chocolate from the heat and pour it onto the rectangle on the parchment. Using an offset spatula, spread the chocolate to fill in the rectangle. Chill until set, about 15 minutes. • While the chocolate is setting, in the same bowl you used to melt the bittersweet chocolate, combine the semisweet chocolate, cream, and peppermint extract. Warm it over the barely simmering water, stirring frequently, until the mixture is just melted and smooth. Remove the bowl from the heat and let the mixture cool until it is room temperature, about 15 minutes. Remove the sheet pan from the refrigerator and pour the semisweet chocolate mixture over the chilled chocolate rectangle. Using an offset spatula, spread the semisweet chocolate in an even layer, then chill until very cold and firm, about 1 hour. • In a clean bowl, warm the white chocolate over barely simmering water until the chocolate is smooth. Working quickly, pour the white chocolate over the firm semisweet layer, using a clean offset spatula to spread it to cover. Sprinkle with the crushed candy canes. Chill in the refrigerator just until firm, about 20 minutes. • Carefully transfer the parchment paper from the sheet pan to a large cutting board. Trim away any uneven edges of the bark so the sides are straight. Cut the bark into 2 by 9 in [5 by 23 cm] wide strips, then cut the strips into squares or triangles. • Let the bark stand at room temperature for 10 minutes before serving. Store in an airtight container, layering sheets of wax paper or parchment paper between the layers so the pieces don't stick to one another, in the refrigerator for up to 1 week.

Triple Chocolate Peppermint Bark

Red Velvet Crinkle Cookies

I rarely try to make my holiday cookies in red and green colors, but every once in a while I submit to tradition. These cookies are actually a shade of burgundy (how I like my red velvet to be), but you can add extra red food coloring if you want them to be more vibrant.

1½ cups [213 g] all-purpose flour	½ cup [100 g] light brown sugar	1 tablespoon Red Velvet Bakery Emulsion or red food coloring	3 oz [85 g] semisweet or bittersweet chocolate
1 teaspoon baking powder	2 large eggs plus 2 large egg yolks, at room temperature	1 teaspoon pure vanilla extract	¼ cup [25 g] cocoa powder
⅛ teaspoon baking soda	1 tablespoon canola oil	½ teaspoon salt	½ cup [60 g] confectioners' sugar
¾ cup plus 3 tablespoons [188 g] granulated sugar		4 tablespoons [57 g] unsalted butter	

127

Adjust an oven rack to the middle position and preheat the oven to 350°F [180°C]. Line three sheet pans with parchment paper. • In a small bowl, whisk together the flour, baking powder, and baking soda. • In a large bowl, whisk together ¾ cup [150 g] of the granulated sugar, the brown sugar, eggs, egg yolks, canola oil, Red Velvet Bakery Emulsion, vanilla, and salt. • Place the butter and chocolate in a small, heavy-bottom saucepan over low heat and melt together, stirring frequently to prevent the chocolate from scorching.

continued

Continue cooking until the mixture is smooth. Off the heat, add the cocoa powder to the chocolate and whisk until completely combined, about 45 seconds (the mixture will be thick). • Add the warm chocolate-butter mixture to the egg mixture and whisk together until combined. Add the flour mixture and use a rubber spatula to mix gently until combined. Cover the dough and chill the mixture for at least 6 hours and up to overnight. • In a small bowl, combine the confectioners' sugar and the remaining 3 tablespoons of granulated sugar. Scoop the dough into 1½ tablespoon portions (see note) and roll the dough in the sugar mixture. Place eight cookies on each sheet pan and bake one pan at a time, rotating halfway through baking. Bake until the edges are set and the cookies are puffed but still soft in the center, 12 to 14 minutes. Move the sheet pans to a wire rack and let the cookies cool to room temperature. Cookies can be stored in an airtight container at room temperature for up to 3 days.

NOTE

The dough is very sticky, so using a cookie scoop works best here; I like to drop the dough balls into the powdered sugar and then gently roll them. Once they are covered, they are easy to pick up. If you don't have a cookie scoop, you can refrigerate the dough for 15 minutes or so to help it scoop more easily.

Red Velvet Crinkle Cookies

Turtle Bars

Every year my mom made several variations of "turtle bars" around the holidays—recipes found in our ancient church cookbook that often turned out to be either a basic seven-layer bar (with a graham cracker crust, shredded coconut, and chocolate) or bars made with layers of pretzels, caramel candies, and pecans. They were family favorites, regardless of the combination. I decided to come up with my own variation; my family still asks for them each year. I still call them Turtle Bars, in honor of my mom, and because they still hit all the right chocolate-caramel-pecan notes.

CRUST

1 cup [2 sticks or 227 g] unsalted butter, at room temperature

1 cup [200 g] granulated sugar

½ teaspoon salt

1 large egg

1 teaspoon pure vanilla extract

2 cups [284 g] all-purpose flour

2 cups [360 g] chocolate chips

CARAMEL

1½ cups [300 g] granulated sugar

¼ teaspoon salt

¼ cup [60 g] water

3 tablespoons corn syrup

¼ cup plus 3 tablespoons [105 g] heavy cream

2 tablespoons unsalted butter

1 teaspoon pure vanilla extract

ASSEMBLY

2 cups [280 g] toasted pecan halves

129

FOR THE CRUST

Adjust an oven rack to the middle position and preheat the oven to 350°F [180°C]. Grease a 9 by 13 in [23 by 33 cm] pan and line it with a parchment sling (see page 16). • In the bowl of a stand mixer fitted with a paddle, beat the butter on medium speed until creamy, about 1 minute. Add the sugar and salt and mix on medium speed until light and creamy, 2 to 3 minutes.

continued

Add the egg and vanilla and mix on low speed until combined. Add the flour and mix on low speed until combined. Press the mixture into the prepared pan. Bake for 18 to 22 minutes, until the shortbread is golden brown. Remove the pan from the oven and scatter the chocolate chips over the hot crust. Return to the oven and bake for 2 minutes. Remove the pan and use an offset spatula to carefully spread the chocolate evenly over the crust. Transfer the pan to a wire rack and let sit at room temperature until the chocolate is set.

FOR THE CARAMEL

In a large, heavy-bottom saucepan, combine the sugar, salt, water, and corn syrup, stirring very gently to combine while trying to avoid getting any sugar crystals on the sides of the pan. Cover the pot and bring to a boil over medium-high heat until the sugar has melted and the mixture is clear, 3 to 5 minutes. Uncover and cook until the sugar has turned a pale golden color and registers about 300°F [150°C] on an instant-read thermometer, 4 to 5 minutes. Turn the heat down slightly and cook for a few minutes more until the sugar is golden and registers 350°F [180°C]. Immediately remove the pan from the heat and add the heavy cream. The cream will foam considerably, so be careful pouring it in. Add the butter next, followed by the vanilla, and stir to combine. Set aside to cool for 5 to 10 minutes.

TO ASSEMBLE

Pour the caramel over the cooled shortbread and set chocolate, using an offset spatula to smooth it evenly. Press the pecan halves into the caramel. Let set at room temperature before slicing. Bars can be stored in an airtight container in the refrigerator for 2 or 3 days.

Chocolate Gift Cakes

In my first book, I had a recipe for picnic cakes—three little cakes that could be packed up and taken on the road or passed out to friends and neighbors. I came up with this chocolate version for the winter months: two for giving, one for keeping.

CHOCOLATE CAKE

½ cup [120 g] sour cream, at room temperature

½ cup [120 g] whole milk, at room temperature

½ cup [112 g] canola oil

3 large eggs, at room temperature

1 teaspoon pure vanilla extract

2 cups [284 g] all-purpose flour

1 cup [200 g] granulated sugar

1 cup [200 g] light brown sugar

¾ cup [75 g] Dutch-process cocoa powder

2 teaspoons baking soda

1 teaspoon baking powder

1 teaspoon salt

1 cup [240 g] strong, freshly brewed coffee, hot

CHOCOLATE BUTTERCREAM

8 oz [226 g] semisweet or bittersweet chocolate

1½ cups [3 sticks or 339 g] unsalted butter, at room temperature

Pinch salt

3 tablespoons corn syrup

2 teaspoons pure vanilla extract

2 cups [240 g] confectioners' sugar

FOR THE CAKE

Adjust an oven rack to the middle position and preheat the oven to 350°F [180°C]. Grease three 6 by 2 in [15 by 5 cm] cake pans and line the bottoms with parchment paper (see page 16).

continued

In a medium bowl or liquid measuring cup, combine the sour cream, milk, oil, eggs, and vanilla. • In the bowl of a stand mixer fitted with a paddle, combine the flour, granulated and brown sugars, cocoa powder, baking soda, baking powder, and salt. • With the mixer running on low speed, slowly add the milk mixture. Increase the speed to medium and beat until combined, 20 to 30 seconds. Slowly pour the hot coffee into the batter and mix until just combined. Using a spatula, give the batter a couple of turns to make sure it is fully mixed. • Divide the batter evenly between the prepared pans. Bake for 25 to 35 minutes, until a wooden skewer or toothpick come out with the tiniest bit of crumb. • Transfer the cakes to a wire rack and let cool for 30 minutes. Turn the cakes out onto the rack, remove the parchment paper, and let cool completely. Once cool, the cakes can be frosted or wrapped in plastic wrap and refrigerated overnight.

FOR THE CHOCOLATE BUTTERCREAM

Pour 1 in [5 cm] of water into a medium saucepan over medium heat and bring it to a gentle boil. • Melt the chocolate in a heatproof bowl set over the pan of boiling water, being careful not to let the water touch the bottom of the bowl. Stir constantly until just melted and set aside to cool slightly. • In the bowl of a stand mixer fitted with a paddle, beat the butter and salt on medium speed until light yellow and fluffy, about 3 minutes. Add the corn syrup and vanilla and beat on medium speed until combined. Lower the speed to low and gradually add the confectioners' sugar. Beat on medium speed, stopping to scrape down the sides of the bowl as necessary, until smooth and creamy, 2 to 3 minutes. Add the chocolate and mix on low speed until no streaks remain. Use a rubber spatula to mix the frosting a few more times, making sure it is completely combined.

TO ASSEMBLE

Divide the chocolate icing between the three cakes and spread it evenly over the tops of the cakes with an offset spatula. The cakes can be covered and stored in the refrigerator for 24 hours. Bring to room temperature before serving.

Modern Fruit Cakes

I've always loved the history and tradition behind fruit cakes, but I've never actually been moved by any of the ones I tried, finding them to be overly dry or quite liquored up. I decided to come up with a "modern" version, one that loosely fits the term *fruit cake* but still gives a loving nod to all the ones before it. While experimenting with recipes, I came across a photo for a fruit cake cookie on the Martha Stewart website that was exactly how I had envisioned my cakes to look. Highly inspired, I went back to the kitchen and came up with a cake version, enhanced with almond and orange and cherry, then covered in chocolate and topped with a gold leaf.

CANDIED CHERRIES

1½ cups [300 g] granulated sugar

3 tablespoons kirsch

¼ teaspoon salt

2 cups [280 g] frozen sour cherries, thawed overnight in a plastic bag and juices saved, (see note, page 136)

CAKE

½ cup [105 g] egg whites (from 3 or 4 large eggs)

½ cup [120 g] whole milk, at room temperature

2 tablespoons Crème Fraîche (page 205) or sour cream, at room temperature

1 tablespoon triple sec

1½ teaspoons pure vanilla extract

1 teaspoon almond extract

1⅓ cups plus 1 tablespoon [199 g] all-purpose flour

1 cup [200 g] granulated sugar

1 tablespoon orange zest

2 teaspoons baking powder

½ teaspoon salt

8 tablespoons [1 stick or 113 g] unsalted butter, at room temperature, cut into 8 pieces, plus more for greasing the pan

½ cup [70 g] Candied Orange Peels (page 201), or store-bought candied peel

½ cup [70 g] dried fruit (such as papaya, apricots, cranberries, etc.; optional)

CHOCOLATE COATING

14 oz [397 g] semisweet or bittersweet chocolate, finely chopped

2 oz [57 g] shortening

Edible gold leaf, for garnish (optional)

135

continued

In a large, heavy-bottom saucepan over medium heat, combine the sugar, kirsch, salt, and cherry juice. Cook until the sugar is dissolved, 3 to 4 minutes. • Add the sour cherries, turn the heat up to medium-high, and bring to a boil. Cover the pan, turn the heat down to medium-low, and let the cherries simmer for 45 minutes, stirring occasionally, until they are wrinkled but slightly firm. The syrup should be at 235°F [113°C] at this point. • Remove the pan from the heat and let cool to room temperature. Once cool, remove the cherries from the liquid and transfer them to a parchment-lined sheet pan if using them immediately, or store in an airtight container in the refrigerator for up to 4 months. The cherry syrup can also be stored in an airtight container in the refrigerator for the same amount of time.

FOR THE CAKE

Adjust an oven rack to the middle position and preheat the oven to 350°F [180°C]. Grease a 9 by 13 in [23 by 33 cm] pan and line it with a parchment sling (see page 16). Line a sheet pan with parchment paper. • In a medium bowl or liquid measuring cup, whisk together the egg whites, milk, crème fraîche, triple sec, vanilla, and almond extract. • In the bowl of a stand mixer fitted with a paddle, combine flour, sugar, orange zest, baking powder, and salt. With the mixer running on low speed, add the butter one piece at a time, beating until the mixture resembles coarse sand. • With the mixer still running on low speed, slowly add the wet ingredients, mixing until just combined. Increase the speed to medium and beat for 30 seconds (the batter may still look a little bumpy). Scrape down the sides and

bottom of the bowl and use a spatula to mix the batter a few more times. Gently stir in the sugar-soaked cherries, orange peel, and dried fruit, if using. • Pour the batter into the prepared pan and smooth the top. Tap the pan gently on the counter twice to help get rid of any air bubbles. Bake for 18 to 24 minutes, rotating the pan halfway through, until the cake is golden brown and a wooden skewer or toothpick inserted into the center comes out with a faint bit of crumbs, or a finger gently pressed into the top leaves a slight indentation. • Transfer the pan to a wire rack and let cool. Wrap the cake, still in the pan, in plastic and let chill in the refrigerator for 2 hours and up to overnight. • Remove the cake from the pan using the parchment sling. Trim off the uneven edges of the cake, then use a 2 in [5 cm] biscuit cutter to cut out circles. Place the cut circles on the prepared sheet pan and transfer it to the freezer while preparing the chocolate.

FOR THE CHOCOLATE COATING

In a small saucepan over low heat, melt 12 oz [340 g] of the chocolate and the shortening, stirring together until smooth. Remove the saucepan from the heat and add the remaining 2 oz [57 g] of chocolate, stirring until melted and completely smooth.

TO ASSEMBLE

Line a sheet pan with parchment paper and set a greased wire rack over it. Take one piece of cake out of the freezer at a time and place it on a fork. Spoon the melted chocolate over the top, allowing it to coat the entire cake and allowing any excess to drip back into the saucepan. Place the cake on the wire rack and repeat with the remaining cakes. Let the cakes stand at room temperature until set. If desired, decorate with a few flecks of edible gold leaf. Store cakes in an airtight container at room temperature for up to 2 days.

NOTE

The cherries should leak quite a bit of juice when they thaw overnight, but if they don't, add ½ cup [120 g] of water to the saucepan.

Florentines

For several years, over winter break, I would come home from college and spend almost every waking second working at a coffee shop located in a nearby mall. Online shopping was not yet a way of life, so the malls would be packed with people desperately looking for gifts. Our coffee shop was the only place to get espresso-laced drinks in the mall (lattes were also just becoming a way of life) and we would have a line trailing out of the store from open to close each day; tired shoppers ordering half-caff lattes with seven different flavor shots or blended mochas for their group of twenty. Our store would receive packages of Florentines each Christmas season to sell, and I have a vivid memory of a woman coming in every day for a week, buying up all the packages we would put out. Each day, she would talk about her yearly trips to Italy, letting us know we just *had* to summer in Italy and we just *had* to try these cookies. I would ring up her order, watching her tear open a bag each time, nibbling on the cookies and spilling crumbs all over the counter, trying my best to conjure up holiday cheer while lamenting that I had never been to Europe.

Even with such a positive review, I never tried Florentines until years later, and discovered they were really quite delicious—delicious enough to understand the raving and the scattered crumbs. My version here is inspired by Thomas Keller and Sebastien Rouxel's *Bouchon Bakery*; the Florentines are made in a huge rectangle, with a pâte sucrée crust sandwiched between pâte à glacer brune and handmade candied orange peels. I love this approach because it is easy to assemble, but I've simplified things with some bittersweet chocolate and a basic shortbread crust.

12 tablespoons
[1½ sticks or 170 g]
unsalted butter, at
room temperature,
plus more for
greasing the pan

½ cup [100 g]
granulated sugar

½ teaspoon salt

2 teaspoons grated
orange peel

2 large egg yolks, at
room temperature

1 teaspoon pure
vanilla extract

1½ cups [213 g]
all-purpose flour,
plus more for dusting

½ cup [120 g] heavy
cream

⅓ cup [65 g]
granulated sugar

¼ cup [80 g] light
corn syrup

¼ teaspoon salt

4 tablespoons [57 g]
unsalted butter

3 tablespoons
triple sec

1 teaspoon pure
vanilla extract

2 cups [200 g]
sliced almonds

¼ cup [74 g] candied
orange peels,
chopped

10 oz [283 g]
semisweet or
bittersweet
chocolate

FOR THE CRUST

Grease and line the bottom of a quarter sheet pan (9 by 13 by 1 in [23 by 33 by 2.5 cm]) with parchment paper. • In the bowl of a stand mixer fitted with a paddle, beat the butter on low speed until creamy, about 1 minute. Add the sugar, salt, and grated orange peel and beat on medium speed until combined and creamy, 2 to 3 minutes. Add the egg yolks and vanilla and mix again on low speed until combined. Add the flour and mix on low speed until completely combined and the dough starts to form a ball. • Dump the dough out onto a lightly floured work surface and shape it into a rectangle. Transfer the rectangle to the prepared pan and gently press it into the bottom and corners, but not up the sides (this dough is very forgiving, so if it cracks as you are pressing it, you can patch it up as you go). Place a piece of plastic wrap over the top and use it to smooth and even out the surface by pressing on it with your hands. Freeze the dough for 15 minutes, or until firm to the touch. • Adjust an oven rack to the middle position and preheat the oven to 350°F [180°C]. • Remove the pan from the freezer. Completely cover the dough with parchment paper and then place another quarter sheet pan over the top (if you don't have another sheet pan the same size, you can cover the parchment paper with pie weights or uncooked rice). Bake the shortbread for 10 to 15 minutes, until it is pale golden in color. Transfer the pan to a wire rack, remove the top pan (or pie weights), and let the shortbread cool in the pan. Turn the oven temperature down to 325°F [165°C].

139

continued

FOR THE FILLING

While the shortbread is cooling, in a medium saucepan over medium heat, combine the heavy cream, sugar, corn syrup, and salt and cook, stirring occasionally, until the sugar is dissolved. Turn the heat up to medium-high and continue to cook until the mixture bubbles and foams up and then collapses (although still bubbling), and the temperature reaches 248°F [120°C], 5 to 6 minutes. Remove the pan from the heat and add the butter, triple sec, and vanilla, swirling until combined. Add the almonds and candied orange peel and stir to combine.

TO ASSEMBLE

Pour the filling over the cooled crust and spread it evenly with an offset spatula. Transfer the pan to the oven and bake for 25 to 30 minutes, rotating the pan halfway through baking, until the filling is golden brown with no undercooked areas (the edges might get toasty, but they can be trimmed off if needed). • Move the pan to a wire rack to cool and immediately run a spatula or the tip of a knife around the edges to loosen them slightly. Repeat again in 5 minutes. Let cool completely. • In a small saucepan over low heat, melt 8 oz [226 g] of the chocolate, stirring until smooth. Remove the saucepan from the heat and add the remaining 2 oz [57 g] of chocolate, stirring until melted and completely smooth. • Line a sheet pan with parchment paper and set a wire rack over it. Remove the shortbread from the pan and place it filling-side down on the wire rack. Pour the melted chocolate over the shortbread crust and spread it in an even layer to cover the whole crust. If desired, use a plastic baking comb to make lines in the chocolate. Let stand at room temperature until the chocolate is set. • Using a serrated knife, trim the edges, if desired, and cut the Florentines into twelve or sixteen squares. Florentines are best eaten the day they are made, but can be stored in an airtight container at room temperature for up to 2 days.

Florentines

Vanilla Bean Sablés

I always include various kinds of sablés in my holiday gift-giving boxes—they are simple to make, and a variety of flavors can be added to the basic dough. They really are the perfect slice-and-bake treat. Use European-style butter instead of the unsalted to make these extra buttery.

1 cup [2 sticks or 227 g] unsalted butter, at room temperature

⅔ cup [130 g] granulated sugar, plus more for sprinkling

⅓ cup [40 g] confectioners' sugar

1 teaspoon salt

1 vanilla bean, seeds scraped, or 1 teaspoon pure vanilla extract

2 large egg yolks

2 cups [284 g] all-purpose flour, plus more for dusting

1 cup [200 g] turbinado or sanding sugar, for sprinkling

In the bowl of a stand mixer fitted with a paddle, beat the butter on medium speed until creamy, about 1 minute. Add the granulated and confectioners' sugars, salt, and vanilla bean seeds, if using, and beat again on medium speed until creamy and combined, 2 to 3 minutes. Add the yolks and vanilla extract, if using, and mix on low speed. Add the flour and mix again on low speed until combined. • Lightly dust your work surface with flour and transfer the dough. Form the dough into a 12 in [30.5 cm] log and place the log on a piece of plastic wrap a few inches longer than the log. Sprinkle the turbinado sugar over each side of the log, covering the outside of the dough. Gently press the sugar into the dough with your hands, then wrap the log in the plastic wrap and refrigerate until firm, about 2 hours, or overnight.

143

Gift Giving

continued

Adjust an oven rack to the middle position and preheat the oven to 350°F [180°C]. Line three sheet pans with parchment paper. • Unwrap the chilled log and slice it into ½ in [12 mm] thick rounds, spacing the rounds about 2 in [5 cm] apart on the sheet pans. Bake one pan at a time, rotating the pan halfway through baking, until the edges are very light golden brown but the centers are still pale, 14 to 16 minutes. Transfer the pan to a wire rack and let the cookies cool completely on the pan. Repeat with the remaining cookies. Store cookies in an airtight container at room temperature for up to 3 days.

Citrus

Add 2 teaspoons of grated citrus zest (lemon, lime, orange, or grapefruit) to the dough along with the salt. Add 1 tablespoon of poppy seeds along with the flour, if desired.

Rosemary Chocolate Chip

Add ½ cup [90 g] of mini chocolate chips (or finely chopped chocolate) and 2 teaspoons of minced rosemary to the dough after incorporating the flour, mixing gently to combine.

Pistachio

Add ⅓ cup [40 g] of chopped pistachios to the dough after incorporating the flour, mixing gently to combine.

Cacao Nib and Caramelized White Chocolate

Add ½ cup [60 g] of chopped cacao nibs and 1 oz [30 g] of finely chopped caramelized white chocolate to the dough after incorporating the flour, mixing gently to combine.

Cut-Out Cookies

Cut-out cookies have been a Christmas tradition in my family since I was a little girl, and while I have many happy memories of cutting out shapes with my mom, I also have plenty of memories of my sister and I fighting over cookie cutters and getting in trouble for hiding all the pretty sprinkles from everyone else. Growing up we never iced our cookies (it was sprinkles all the way), but I've included an icing option here, a simple glaze that is easy to make and tastes delicious. If you prefer, a sugar coating is also an option.

COOKIES

4 cups [568 g] all-purpose flour, plus more for dusting

1 teaspoon salt

¾ teaspoon baking powder

¼ teaspoon baking soda

1½ cups [3 sticks or 339 g] unsalted butter, at room temperature

3 tablespoons refined coconut oil, at room temperature

1¾ cups [350 g] granulated sugar

1 large egg plus 1 large egg yolk, at room temperature

1 tablespoon pure vanilla extract

SIMPLE GLAZE

2 cups [240 g] confectioners' sugar

1 tablespoon unsalted butter, melted

1 teaspoon pure vanilla extract

Pinch salt

3 to 6 tablespoons [45 to 80 g] water

Food coloring (optional)

FREEZE-DRIED SUGAR COATING

1 cup [200 g] granulated sugar

1 to 2 cups [32 to 64 g] freeze-dried berries, such as strawberries or raspberries (add more or less depending on how much flavor and vibrant color you want)

145

FOR THE COOKIES

In a large bowl, whisk together the flour, salt, baking powder, and baking soda. • In the bowl of a stand mixer fitted with a paddle, mix the butter on medium speed until creamy.

continued

Add the coconut oil and mix again on medium speed until smooth. Add the granulated sugar and mix again on medium until light and creamy, 3 to 5 minutes. Add the egg, yolk, and vanilla and mix again on low speed until combined. Add the flour mixture and mix on low speed until completely combined. Use a spatula to fold in any dry pieces of dough that may be lingering on the bottom of the bowl. Divide the dough in half; it can be used immediately or wrapped in plastic and refrigerated for up to 4 days (let the dough come to room temperature before rolling). • Adjust an oven rack to the middle position and preheat the oven to 350°F [180°C]. Line several sheet pans with parchment paper. • On a floured surface, roll out the dough somewhere between ⅛ in [4 mm] and ¼ in [6 mm] thick (the thinner the cookie, the crisper it will be, so this will depend on your preference). Use cookie cutters to cut out shapes, then slide a spatula underneath the dough and transfer the shapes to the sheet pans, leaving 1 in [2.5 cm] of space between the cookies. Chill the pans of cookies in the refrigerator for 15 minutes before baking. Dough scraps can be re-rolled and cut out again. • Bake the cookies, one pan at a time, until cooked through, 12 to 16 minutes. For a softer cookie, bake for 12 minutes; for a crisper

cookie, bake longer, until light golden brown around the edges. Place the baking pans on a wire rack and let the cookies cool completely on the pans before icing. Repeat with the remaining cookies.

FOR THE SIMPLE GLAZE

Place the confectioners' sugar in a medium bowl. Add the melted butter, vanilla, salt, and 3 tablespoons of water and stir to combine. Add food coloring, if using. If the mixture is very thick, add 1 tablespoon of water at a time until the desired consistency is reached. Spread the glaze over the cooled cookies. Once the glaze is set, cookies can be stored in an airtight container at room temperature for up to 3 days.

FOR THE FREEZE-DRIED SUGAR COATING

Place the freeze-dried berries and granulated sugar in a food processor, and process until the berries are finely ground and the sugar and berries are combined, about 30 seconds. Sprinkle the tops of the cookies with the berry-sugar mixture, gently rubbing it into the surface, and shaking off any excess. The sugar-coated cookies can be stored in an airtight container at room temperature for up to 3 days.

4

"It snows in here. It snows forever.
But there's no Christmas underneath
this weather."

—OVER THE RHINE, "JACK'S VALENTINE"

Beyond Christmas

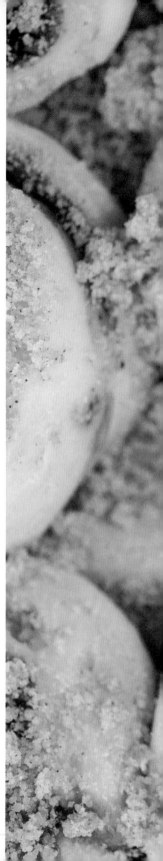

Everything Bundt Cake

This cake evolved from a variety of sources and bakeries I worked in and over many decades of making Bundt cakes in my own kitchen. I've slowly tweaked and fiddled my working recipe, finding my way here, to this Everything Bundt Cake. Sour cream adds a slight tang, and a little canola oil keeps the cake moist over several days. I prefer this cake on the second and third days; the flavor develops and the crumb is tender and perfectly buttery.

3 cups [426 g] all-purpose flour	½ cup [120 g] whole milk, at room temperature	3 cups [600 g] granulated sugar	2 tablespoons canola oil
½ teaspoon baking soda	1¼ cups [2½ sticks or 283 g] unsalted butter, at room temperature, plus more for greasing the pan	1¼ teaspoons salt	1 tablespoon pure vanilla extract
½ cup [120 g] sour cream, at room temperature		6 large eggs, at room temperature	

Adjust an oven rack to the middle position and preheat the oven to 350°F [180°C]. Grease a 10 in [25 cm] tube or Bundt pan (see Quick Tip, page 152). • In a medium bowl, whisk together the flour and baking soda. • In a medium bowl or liquid measuring cup, whisk together the sour cream and whole milk until combined. • In the bowl of a stand mixer fitted with a paddle, beat the butter on medium speed until creamy, about 1 minute. Add the sugar and salt and beat on medium speed until very light and fluffy, 4 to 6 minutes.

continued

Scrape down the sides of the bowl and add the eggs one at a time, beating on medium speed until incorporated and stopping to scrape down the sides of the bowl after each addition. Add the canola oil and vanilla and mix on low speed to combine. Add half of the flour mixture and mix on low speed until combined. Add the sour cream mixture and mix on low speed until combined. Scrape down the sides of the bowl, add the remaining flour mixture, and mix on low speed until combined. Increase the speed to medium and beat for 15 to 20 seconds. • Pour the batter into the prepared pan and use a spatula to even out the top. Bake for 50 to 65 minutes, until a wooden skewer or toothpick inserted near the center comes out clean. • Transfer the pan to a wire rack and gently run a knife around the edge of the cake to loosen it. Let cool for 20 minutes in the pan, then invert the cake onto the rack and remove the pan to finish cooling. The cake can be wrapped in plastic wrap and kept at room temperature for 2 days, or refrigerated for up to 4 days.

QUICK TIP

GREASING A BUNDT PAN

More often than not, when one goes to flip a well-used Bundt pan, part (or half! or all!) of the cake sticks, resulting in disappointment and disaster. If I am making a Bundt cake with lots of add-ins (fruit, nuts, chocolate, etc.), I use a 16 cup [3.8 L] ring pan with a flat bottom and no ridges or design. I generously grease it and then line the bottom with a piece of parchment paper. This has worked perfectly 99.9 percent of the time, and I no longer fear flipping my cooled cake over. I still love my intricate Bundt pans and save those for plain pound cakes.

Confetti

Add ¾ cup [115 g] of sprinkles to the batter after adding
the flour mixture and mix gently until combined.

Cream Cheese

Use 1 cup [2 sticks or 227 g] of unsalted butter and 6 oz [170 g] of
cream cheese, both at room temperature, instead of 1¼ cups [2½ sticks or 300 g]
of butter. Beat the cream cheese with the butter until smooth and creamy,
then add the sugar and other ingredients.

Lemon Poppy Seed

Whisk 3 tablespoons of poppy seeds in with the flour mixture.
Add 2 tablespoons of grated lemon zest along with the sugar, and
replace ¼ cup [60 g] of the whole milk with ¼ cup [60 g] of fresh lemon juice.

Brown Sugar–Chocolate

Replace 2 cups [400 g] of the granulated sugar with brown sugar.
Add 1 cup [180 g] of mini chocolate chips after adding the flour
mixture, and stir gently to combine.

Cardamom

Add 1 tablespoon of ground cardamom to the dry ingredients.

Lemon Pull-Apart Bread

As the name suggests, you just pull apart the bread to eat a slice! This bread is a little time consuming to make but always worth the effort—each piece is coated in butter, lemon, sugar, and icing.

LEMON BREAD

3 large eggs, at room temperature

½ cup [120 g] whole milk, warm (100°F to 110°F [35°C to 45°C])

2 tablespoons honey

1 tablespoon granulated sugar

3 cups plus 2 tablespoons [444 g] all-purpose flour, plus more for dusting

2 teaspoons instant yeast

1½ teaspoons salt

8 tablespoons [1 stick or 113 g] unsalted butter, at room temperature, cut into 8 pieces, plus more for greasing the pan

FILLING

¾ cup [150 g] granulated sugar

2 tablespoons lemon zest

Pinch salt

2 tablespoons unsalted butter, melted and cooled slightly

ICING

1½ cups [180 g] confectioners' sugar

2 to 4 tablespoons [30 to 60 g] fresh lemon juice

1 tablespoon unsalted butter, melted

1 teaspoon pure vanilla extract

FOR THE BREAD

Grease a large bowl and set aside. • In a large liquid measuring cup, combine the eggs, milk, honey, and granulated sugar. • In the bowl of a stand mixer fitted with a paddle, mix together the flour, yeast, and salt on low speed to combine.

continued

Add the egg mixture and mix on low speed to combine (if the mixture is dry and some of the flour isn't combining, add 1 to 2 tablespoons of water—but no more—to help incorporate it). • With the mixer running on low speed, add the butter one piece at a time. When all the butter has been added, increase the speed to medium and beat the butter into the dough until all the little butter pieces are incorporated, about 1 minute. Transfer the dough to the prepared bowl; the dough will be sticky and you will need a spatula to scrape it into the bowl. • Cover the bowl with plastic wrap and let the dough rise for 30 minutes. Remove the plastic wrap and place your fingers or a spatula underneath the dough to gently pull the dough up and fold it back over itself. Turn the bowl slightly and repeat this folding. Repeat this folding motion six to eight more times until all the dough has been folded over on itself. *See how-to photos, page 77.* Re-cover the bowl with plastic wrap and let the dough rise for 30 minutes. Repeat this series of folding three more times, for a rise time of 2 hours and a total of four foldings. Tightly cover the bowl with plastic wrap and refrigerate overnight or for up to 72 hours.

FOR THE FILLING

In a small bowl, mix together the granulated sugar, lemon zest, and salt.

TO BAKE

Adjust an oven rack to the middle position and preheat the oven to 350°F [180°C]. Line a 9 by 4 by 4 in [23 by 10 by 10 cm] Pullman pan with a sling (see page 16). • Lightly flour your work surface, then roll the dough into a 20 by 12 in [50 by 30.5 cm] rectangle with a short edge facing you. With a pastry brush, spread the melted butter evenly over the dough. Sprinkle the lemon-sugar mixture over the dough

and press it gently into the dough with your hands. • Using a pastry wheel or pizza cutter, cut the dough crosswise into five strips (about 12 by 4 in [30.5 by 10 cm]) each, then stack the five rectangles on top of each other. • Slice the stack of rectangles to create six equal strips, about 4 by 2 in [10 by 5 cm] each. Fit these layered strips into the prepared loaf pan, cut-edges up and side by side (it will be a tight fit, but it is okay to press them close together). *See how-to photos, pages 158–159.* Loosely cover the pan with plastic wrap and let the dough rise in a warm place until almost doubled in size, 45 to 60 minutes. (Bread can also do a slow rise in the refrigerator overnight, see Make It Early, facing page) • Place a sheet pan on a lower oven rack (this will help catch any drips). Bake the bread until the top is golden brown, 40 to 50 minutes, or registers 195°F [91°C] on an instant-read thermometer. Check the bread halfway through baking—if the top is browning too quickly, cover it with a piece of foil.

FOR THE ICING

While the bread is baking, whisk together the confectioners' sugar, 2 tablespoons of the lemon juice, the melted butter, and vanilla until smooth. Add more lemon juice, 1 tablespoon at a time, to thin the icing to your preferred consistency.

TO ASSEMBLE

Transfer the loaf pan to a wire rack and immediately pour half of the icing over the bread, then let sit for 15 minutes. Use the sling to gently remove the loaf from the pan, then drizzle the remaining icing over the loaf. Let cool slightly before pulling apart and eating. This bread is best eaten the day it's made.

Lemon Pull-Apart Bread

Prepare the Lemon Pull-Apart Bread, but do not let rise for 45 minutes as stated in the main recipe. Instead, cover the pan loosely with plastic wrap and refrigerate for up to 18 hours. When ready to bake, preheat the oven and let the bread sit at room temperature (still covered in plastic) for 45 minutes to 1 hour. Bake as directed.

VARIATIONS

Cinnamon Pull-Apart Bread

Omit the lemon zest from the filling and replace it with 2 tablespoons of ground cinnamon. Omit the lemon juice from the icing and replace it with water.

Orange Pull-Apart Bread

Replace the lemon zest and juice with orange zest and juice.

Blood Orange Turnovers

These turnovers can be as labor-intensive or as quick and easy as you desire. I prefer them made with homemade Rough Puff Pastry, but store-bought will also work. If you don't have time to make the Blood Orange Curd (page 209), any jam of your choice can replace it in a pinch. I always include the creamy Cream Cheese Filling, but it can be omitted.

CREAM CHEESE FILLING

4 oz [113 g] cream cheese, at room temperature

2 tablespoons granulated sugar

½ teaspoon pure vanilla extract

Pinch salt

1 teaspoon fresh lemon juice

ASSEMBLY

All-purpose flour, for dusting

1 recipe Rough Puff Pastry (page 186), cut into two pieces, or 1 lb [454 g] store-bought puff pastry

½ cup [160 g] Blood Orange Curd (page 209)

Egg wash (see page 16)

Granulated sugar, for sprinkling

FOR THE CREAM CHEESE FILLING

In the bowl of a stand mixer fitted with a paddle, beat together the cream cheese, sugar, vanilla, and salt on low speed until smooth, about 1 minute. Scrape down the sides of the bowl, add ¼ teaspoon of the lemon juice, and mix on low speed to combine. Taste the filling—you are looking for the lemon juice to brighten the filling, but not make it taste like lemon. Add more juice if needed. Transfer to a bowl, cover with plastic, and refrigerate until ready to use.

TO ASSEMBLE

Adjust an oven rack to the middle position and preheat the oven to 400°F [200°C]. Stack two sheet pans on top of each other and line the top sheet with parchment paper (this helps keep the bottoms of the turnovers from browning too quickly). • Lightly flour a work surface and roll each piece of the dough into a 10 in [25 cm] square. • Cut each square into four 5 in [12 cm] squares, for a total of eight squares. • Place a dollop of filling and a tablespoon of curd in the middle of each square. • Fold each square of dough to make a triangle and crimp the edges with a fork to seal. Transfer the triangles to the prepared sheet pan and freeze for 15 minutes. • Brush the tops of the turnovers lightly with egg wash and generously sprinkle the tops with sugar. Bake the turnovers until golden brown, rotating the pan halfway through, 20 to 25 minutes. Remove the pan from the oven and, using a spatula, transfer the turnovers to a wire rack to cool slightly. Serve warm. Turnovers are best eaten the same day they are made.

Passion Fruit–Poppy Seed Muffins

I discovered my white cake base works for so many applications, but it has also become my favorite muffin—especially when I am looking for a rich, glazed, coffeehouse-style muffin. Here is my passion fruit edition, along with several more variations for you to try.

MUFFINS

1 scant cup [210 g] large egg whites, from 6 or 7 eggs, at room temperature

¾ cup [180 g] sour cream, at room temperature

¾ cup [180 g] passion fruit purée, at room temperature

1 tablespoon pure vanilla extract

2¾ cups [391 g] all-purpose flour

2 cups [400 g] granulated sugar

4 teaspoons baking powder

1 teaspoon salt

1 cup [2 sticks or 227 g] unsalted butter, at room temperature, cut into 1 in [2.5 cm] pieces

2 tablespoons poppy seeds, plus more for sprinkling

PASSION FRUIT ICING

1½ cups [180 g] confectioners' sugar

2 to 4 tablespoons [30 to 60 g] passion fruit purée

1 tablespoon unsalted butter, melted

½ teaspoon pure vanilla extract

163

FOR THE MUFFINS

Adjust an oven rack to the middle position and preheat the oven to 350°F [180°C]. Grease or place liners in two large six-cup muffin tins. • In a medium bowl or liquid measuring cup, whisk together the egg whites, sour cream, passion fruit purée, and vanilla. • In the bowl of a stand mixer fitted with a paddle, combine the flour, granulated sugar, baking powder, and salt. With the mixer running on low speed, add the butter one piece at a time, beating until the mixture resembles coarse sand.

Beyond Christmas

continued

With the mixer still running on low speed, slowly add a little more than half the wet ingredients. Increase the speed to medium and beat until the ingredients are incorporated, about 30 seconds. With the mixer running on low speed, add the rest of the wet ingredients, mixing until just combined. Increase the speed to medium and beat for 20 seconds (the batter may still look a little bumpy). Scrape down the sides and bottom of the bowl, add the poppy seeds, and use a spatula to mix the batter a few more times. • Divide the batter between the muffin cups; the batter should come ½ in [12 mm] below the top. Tap the pans gently on the counter twice to help get rid of any air bubbles. Bake for 22 to 27 minutes, rotating the pans halfway through, until the muffins are golden brown and a wooden skewer or toothpick inserted into the centers comes out with a faint bit of crumbs, or a finger gently pressed into the top leaves a slight indentation.

FOR THE ICING

While the muffins are baking, in a medium bowl, whisk together the confectioners' sugar, 2 tablespoons of the passion fruit purée, the melted butter, and vanilla until smooth. Add more purée, 1 tablespoon at a time, to thin the icing to your preferred consistency. • When the muffins are done baking, transfer the tins to a wire rack and let the muffins cool for 5 minutes. Pour half the icing over the tops of the muffins before removing them from the tins, then transfer them to a wire rack set over a sheet pan lined with parchment paper. Pour the remaining icing over the muffins, sprinkle with additional poppy seeds, and let cool completely. The muffins are best eaten the same day they are made, but can be stored in an airtight container at room temperature for 2 days.

VARIATIONS

Lemon Poppyseed

Replace the passion fruit purée with ½ cup [120 g] of whole milk and ¼ cup [60 g] of fresh lemon juice. Add 1 tablespoon of lemon zest along with the sugar. Replace the passion fruit purée with lemon juice in the icing.

Orange Cranberry

Replace the passion fruit purée with ½ cup [120 g] of whole milk and ¼ cup [60 g] of orange juice. Add 1 tablespoon of orange zest along with the sugar. Add 2 oz [57g] of chopped fresh or frozen (but thawed) cranberries to the batter after combining, gently stirring to incorporate.

Meyer Lemon–White Chocolate Scones

I have made so many thousands of scones over the years, both at home and at various bakeries and coffeehouses I've worked at. My recipe is always evolving and changing, and here is where I have currently landed. I prefer crème fraîche over sour cream, but either will work. If you are unable to find Meyer lemons, regular lemons can be substituted.

SCONES

⅓ cup [65 g] granulated sugar, plus more for sprinkling

2 tablespoons Meyer lemon zest

2¼ cups [320 g] all-purpose flour, plus more for dusting

1 tablespoon baking powder

½ teaspoon salt

½ cup [120 g] Crème Fraîche (page 205) or sour cream

¼ cup [60 g] fresh Meyer lemon juice

1 large egg plus 1 large egg yolk

1 teaspoon pure vanilla extract

12 tablespoons [1½ sticks or 170 g] unsalted butter, cut into 12 pieces and placed in the freezer for 10 minutes

2 oz [55 g] white chocolate, chopped into small pieces

Heavy cream, for brushing

LEMON GLAZE

1½ cups [180 g] confectioners' sugar

2 to 4 tablespoons [30 to 60 g] fresh Meyer lemon juice

1 tablespoon unsalted butter, melted

165

Beyond Christmas

Adjust an oven rack to the middle position and preheat the oven to 400°F [200°C]. Stack two sheet pans on top of each other and line the top sheet with parchment paper (this helps keep the bottoms of the scones from browning too quickly). • In a large bowl, combine the sugar and lemon zest with your hands, rubbing the zest into the sugar. Add the flour, baking powder, and salt and whisk to combine.

continued

In a medium bowl or liquid measuring cup, whisk together the crème fraîche, lemon juice, egg, egg yolk, and vanilla. • Add the butter to the dry ingredients and use a pastry cutter to cut in the butter until the flour-coated pieces are the size of peas. • Add the wet ingredients and fold with a spatula until just combined. Add the white chocolate, gently folding it into the dough. • Transfer the dough to a lightly floured surface and knead four to six times, until it comes together, adding more flour as necessary, as the dough will be sticky. Pat the dough gently into a square and roll it into a 12 in [30.5 cm] square (again, dusting with flour as necessary). Fold the dough in thirds, similar to a business letter. Fold the short ends of the dough in thirds again, making a square. Transfer it to a floured sheet pan or plate and place it in the freezer for 10 minutes. • Return the dough to the floured surface, roll it into a 12 in [30.5 cm] square, and fold it in thirds. Place the dough seam-side down and gently roll the dough into a 12 by 4 in [30.5 by 10 cm] rectangle. With a sharp knife, cut it crosswise into four equal rectangles, then cut each rectangle diagonally into two triangles. Transfer the triangles to the prepared sheet pan. • Brush the tops of the triangles with a little heavy cream, making sure it doesn't drip down the sides, and sprinkle the tops generously with sugar. Bake for 18 to 25 minutes, rotating the pan halfway through, until the tops and bottoms are light golden brown. Transfer the sheet pan to a wire rack and let the scones cool for 5 minutes before glazing.

FOR THE GLAZE

While the scones are baking, in a medium bowl, whisk together the confectioners' sugar, 2 tablespoons of the lemon juice, and the melted butter until smooth. Add more juice, 1 tablespoon at a time, to thin the glaze to your preferred consistency. • Pour the glaze over the tops of the scones and use an offset spatula to smooth the tops. Let set before serving. Scones are best eaten the same day they are made.

MAKE IT EARLY

TO FREEZE SCONES

Once the unbaked scones are cut into triangles, freeze them in a single layer on a sheet pan. Once the scones are frozen solid, transfer them to a freezer-safe bag. They will keep in the freezer for 2 weeks.

Blueberry Streusel Buns

Often on long winter days, when we're far removed from Christmas but not close to spring, I find myself craving summer berries. Knowing that any found in the grocery store aisle won't spark joy until closer to June, I turn to berries tucked away somewhere in my freezer. This is a lovely way to start a dreary morning: a quick blueberry jam rolled in sweet dough, then covered in streusel and icing. Store-bought jam can also be used with good results.

BLUEBERRY JAM

1½ cups [210 g] blueberries, fresh or frozen

¼ cup [50 g] granulated sugar

Pinch salt

1 teaspoon pure vanilla extract

1 teaspoon fresh lemon juice (optional)

BUNS

All-purpose flour, for dusting

1 recipe Sweet Dough (page 76), chilled

2 tablespoons unsalted butter, melted, plus more for greasing

½ recipe Streusel (page 203)

ICING

2 oz [57 g] cream cheese, at room temperature

2 to 4 tablespoons [30 to 60 g] fresh lemon juice or water

1 tablespoon unsalted butter, melted

½ teaspoon pure vanilla extract

Pinch salt

1½ cups [180 g] confectioners' sugar

169

·

Beyond Christmas

FOR THE JAM

In a medium pan over medium heat, simmer the blueberries, granulated sugar, and salt for 20 to 30 minutes, stirring often, until the blueberries have broken down and the jam has thickened. The jam will cling to a wooden spoon when it is done.

continued

Remove the pan from the heat, stir in the vanilla, and allow to cool to room temperature. Taste the jam—if it is a little flat, you can add the lemon juice, about ½ teaspoon at a time, until it brightens the flavor.

TO MAKE THE BUNS

Line a sheet pan with parchment paper. Flour a work surface and knead the cold Sweet Dough ten to twelve times. Shape the dough into a ball, dust the top lightly with flour, cover with a kitchen towel, and let the dough come to room temperature. • Grease a 9 by 13 in [23 by 33 cm] pan; if desired, line it with a parchment (see page 16). • Roll the dough into a 16 by 12 in [40.5 by 30.5 cm] rectangle. Brush the dough with the melted butter and spread ¾ cup [225 g] of the jam evenly over the top. • Starting at a long side, roll the dough into a tight cylinder. Pinch the seam gently to seal it and position the dough seam-side down. Place the roll on the prepared sheet pan and transfer it to the refrigerator to chill for 15 minutes (this makes cutting the buns a little less messy). • Remove the pan from the refrigerator, place the dough log on a cutting board, and use scissors or a sharp knife to cut the dough into twelve equal pieces. Transfer the pieces to the prepared sheet pan and place them cut-side up. Cover the pan loosely with plastic wrap and let the dough

rise at room temperature until doubled, 1 to 1½ hours. • Adjust an oven rack to the middle position and preheat the oven to 350°F [180°C]. Remove the plastic wrap and generously cover the tops of the buns with the streusel, gently pressing the streusel into the buns (there will be some streusel left over). Transfer the sheet pan to the oven and bake for 27 to 32 minutes, rotating the pan halfway through, until the rolls are golden brown.

FOR THE ICING

While the rolls are baking, in a medium bowl, whisk together the cream cheese, 2 tablespoons of the lemon juice, the melted butter, vanilla, and salt until smooth. Add the confectioners' sugar and mix again until smooth. Add more lemon juice, 1 tablespoon at a time, to thin the icing to your preferred consistency. • When the buns have finished baking, transfer the pan to a wire rack and let the buns cools for 10 to 15 minutes, then drizzle evenly with the icing. The buns are best eaten the same day they are made.

NOTE

For a flavor bump, pulse ¼ cup [8 g] freeze-dried blueberries in a food processor, process until powdered, and add them to the pan along with the blueberries as you're making the jam.

Blueberry Streusel Buns

Coconut-Cardamom Cupcakes

These pretty white cupcakes topped with coconut flakes always bring to mind endless winter days. I like to make the cupcakes in popover pans—I'm partial to the tall, straight lines—however, a regular muffin tin will also work just fine.

COCONUT CUPCAKES

1 scant cup [210 g] large egg whites (from 6 or 7 eggs), at room temperature

1 cup [240 g] coconut milk, at room temperature

½ cup [120 g] Crème Fraîche (page 205) or sour cream, at room temperature

1 tablespoon pure vanilla extract

1 teaspoon coconut extract

2¾ cups [391 g] all-purpose flour

2 cups [400 g] granulated sugar

4 teaspoons baking powder

1 teaspoon salt

1 cup [2 sticks or 227 g] unsalted butter, at room temperature, cut into 1 in [2.5 cm] pieces

CARDAMOM BUTTERCREAM

1 cup [2 sticks or 227 g] unsalted butter, at room temperature

8 oz [226 g] cream cheese, at room temperature

2 tablespoons light corn syrup

1 teaspoon ground cardamom

Pinch salt

4½ cups [540 g] confectioners' sugar (see note, page 172)

2 teaspoons pure vanilla extract

ASSEMBLY

Unsweetened coconut flakes, for sprinkling

FOR THE CUPCAKES

Adjust an oven rack to the middle position and preheat the oven to 350°F [180°C]. Grease two large six-cup popover pans or place liners in two standard twelve-cup muffin tins.

continued

171

Beyond Christmas

In a medium bowl or liquid measuring cup, whisk together the egg whites, coconut milk, crème fraîche, vanilla, and coconut extract. • In the bowl of a stand mixer fitted with a paddle, whisk together the flour, granulated sugar, baking powder, and salt by hand until combined. With the mixer running on low speed, add the butter one piece at a time, beating until the mixture resembles coarse sand. With the mixer still running on low speed, slowly add a little more than half of the wet ingredients. Increase the speed to medium and beat until the ingredients are incorporated, about 30 seconds. With the mixer running on low speed, add the rest of the wet ingredients, mixing until just combined. Increase the speed to medium and beat for 20 seconds (the batter may still look a little bumpy). Scrape down the sides and bottom of the bowl and use a spatula to mix the batter a few more times. • Divide the batter between the popover cups, filling them only three-quarters of the way full. Tap the pans gently on the counter twice to help get rid of any air bubbles. Bake for 16 to 22 minutes, rotating the pans halfway through, until the cupcakes are golden brown and a wooden skewer or toothpick inserted into the center comes out with a faint bit of crumbs, or a finger gently pressed into the top leaves a slight indentation. • Transfer the pans to a wire rack and let cool for 15 minutes, then remove the cupcakes from the pans and let cool completely.

FOR THE BUTTERCREAM

In the bowl of a stand mixer fitted with a paddle, beat the butter on medium speed until very creamy, 2 to 3 minutes. Add the cream cheese, corn syrup, cardamom, and salt and mix on medium speed until smooth and creamy, 2 minutes more. With the mixer running on low speed, slowly add the confectioners' sugar, mixing until combined, and scraping down the sides of the bowl as needed. Add the vanilla and mix until combined.

TO ASSEMBLE

Frost each cupcake with a heaping layer of Cardamom Buttercream and top with coconut flakes. Cupcakes can be covered and stored in the refrigerator for 24 hours. Bring to room temperature before serving.

NOTE

The frosting will be a little loose, and isn't a good one for piping. If you want a stiffer icing, you can add more confectioners' sugar, but note that the more you add, the sweeter the frosting will be.

Cruffins

Cruffins are the love child of croissants and muffins and make for a tall, flaky, extravagant morning bun. It appears the first cruffin was made in 2013, created by Kate Reid for a bakery in Melbourne, Australia, then found its way around the world. Cruffins are tedious, but a perfect winter project. I spent hours researching and testing different methods for making them, and finally landed on the recipe below, which is a hybrid of my own croissant dough, a popover pan for height, and a mix of ingenious rolling methods from across the interwebs. For the best flavor, let the cruffins rise overnight in the refrigerator.

All-purpose flour, for dusting 1 recipe Cheater's Croissant Dough (page 70)	3 tablespoons unsalted butter, melted, plus more for greasing the pans	¾ cup [150 g] granulated sugar, plus more for sprinkling in the pan and rolling	Pastry Cream (page 199, optional)

Butter the wells of two large six-cup popover pans, then generously dust each well with sugar. Line a sheet pan with parchment paper. • Place the dough on a lightly floured work surface and cut it into six equal pieces. Place the dough on the prepared sheet pan, cover loosely with plastic, and place in the refrigerator. Take one piece out at a time, and roll each piece as long, wide, and thin as you can, about 8 by 18 in [20 by 46 cm]. Brush the piece with melted butter and sprinkle with a heaping tablespoon of sugar, pressing it in gently to adhere. Starting from a short edge, roll up the dough into a log, then cut the log in half lengthwise so the layers of dough and filling are visible (when you are finished rolling out each piece and cutting each log in half you will have twelve pieces total). Fold the dough in half with the layers fanning out so it's in a horseshoe shape, then twist one side of the dough over the other, making a loop.

continued

Place the ends of the dough into one of the wells in the prepared popover pan so the ends are resting on the bottom and the top loop is slightly sticking out. Repeat with the remaining dough. *See how-to photos, facing page.* • Cover the pans loosely with plastic wrap and let the dough rise at room temperature for 2 to 3 hours, until doubled in size. (It should act similarly to a marshmallow when pressed. Cruffins can also do a slow rise in the refrigerator overnight, see Make It Early, below.) • Adjust an oven rack to the middle position and preheat the oven to 400°F [200°C]. Line a sheet pan with parchment paper. • Remove the plastic wrap from the pans and bake the cruffins for 25 to 35 minutes, until they are golden brown. Let the cruffins sit in the pans for 1 to 2 minutes, then flip them out onto the prepared sheet pan. Roll each cruffin in granulated sugar, then move them to a wire rack to finish cooling. • Fill each cruffin with pastry cream, if desired: Fill a piping bag fitted with a plain tip with the pastry cream. Gently push the tip into the top of the cruffin (find a divot or space and place it in there) and fill each cruffin with a tablespoon or two of pastry cream. Cruffins are best eaten on the same day they are made.

MAKE IT EARLY

FOR OVERNIGHT CRUFFINS

Prepare the Cruffins, but do not let rise for 2 to 3 hours as stated in the main recipe. Instead, cover the pans loosely with plastic wrap and refrigerate for at least 8 and up to 18 hours. When ready to bake, preheat the oven and let the buns sit at room temperature (still covered in plastic wrap) until puffy (it should act similarly to a marshmallow when pressed), 1½ to 2 hours. Bake as directed.

Hot Chocolate Cake

Hot chocolate is a beautiful part of our Minnesota winter routine. Blustery autumn day? Hot chocolate by the fire. Eight inches of snow and we can't go to school? Hot chocolate by the fire. Spent three hours shoveling our driveway and sidewalk? Hot chocolate by the fire. My version of hot chocolate is a chocolate cake tunneled with marshmallow filling, then topped with chocolate ganache and toasted marshmallows. I was inspired by Irvin Lin's Nostalgic Marshmallow-Filled Chocolate Cake in his *Marbled, Swirled, and Layered* cookbook, and used his technique for filling the cake.

CAKE

½ cup [120 g] sour cream, at room temperature

½ cup [120 g] whole milk, at room temperature

½ cup [112 g] canola oil

3 large eggs, at room temperature

1 teaspoon pure vanilla extract

2 cups [284 g] all-purpose flour

1 cup [200 g] granulated sugar

1 cup [200 g] light brown sugar

¾ cup [75 g] Dutch-process cocoa powder

2 teaspoons baking soda

1 teaspoon baking powder

1 teaspoon salt

1 cup [240 g] strong, freshly brewed coffee, hot

MARSHMALLOW FLUFF FILLING

8 tablespoons [1 stick or 113 g] unsalted butter, at room temperature

Pinch salt

1 cup [120 g] confectioners' sugar

2 cups [280 g] Marshmallow Fluff (page 210)

2 tablespoons heavy cream

CHOCOLATE GANACHE

8 oz [226 g] semisweet or bittersweet chocolate

½ cup [120 g] heavy cream

Marshmallows (page 192), cut into cubes and toasted

FOR THE CAKE

Adjust an oven rack to the middle position and preheat the oven to 350°F [180°C]. Grease a tube pan (without a removable bottom, see note, page 180) and line the bottom with parchment paper, with a hole cut out in the middle for the tube (see page 16). • In a medium bowl or liquid measuring cup, whisk together the sour cream, milk, oil, eggs, and vanilla. • In the bowl of a stand mixer fitted with a paddle, whisk together the flour, granulated and brown sugars, cocoa powder, baking soda, baking powder, and salt by hand. • With the mixer running on low speed, slowly add the milk mixture. Increase the speed to medium and beat until combined, 20 to 30 seconds. Slowly pour the hot coffee into the batter and mix on low speed until just combined. Using a spatula, give the batter a couple of turns to make sure it is fully mixed. • Pour the batter evenly into the prepared pan and bake for 25 to 35 minutes, until a wooden skewer or toothpick comes out with the tiniest bit of crumbs. • Transfer the cake to a wire rack and let cool in the pan for 1 hour. Turn the cake out onto the rack, remove the parchment paper, and let cool completely. Line a sheet pan with parchment paper. Wrap the cake in plastic wrap, place it on the prepared sheet pan, and chill the cake for at least 2 hours and up to overnight.

FOR THE FILLING

In the bowl of a stand mixer fitted with a paddle, beat the butter and salt on medium speed until creamy, about 1 minute. Add the confectioners' sugar and beat again until smooth and creamy, 3 to 4 minutes. Scrape down the sides and add the marshmallow fluff, beating on low speed until well blended. Add the heavy cream and beat again on low speed until combined. Transfer the filling to a bowl and cover. Chill in the refrigerator for at least 2 hours and up to overnight.

continued

TO FILL

Set the cake rounded-side up on the sheet pan. Using a small paring knife, make a tunnel in the cake by cutting out small curved rectangles (about 2 in long by 1 in wide [5 by 2.5 cm]) into the top of the cake following the curve of the entire cake, directly in the center. Save the pieces of cut-out cake. The tunnel should go down a little more than half the depth of the cake. • Once you go around the entire cake, spoon the chilled marshmallow filling into the tunnel, filling it halfway (you may have some leftover fluff). Cut off half of the inside of each piece of cut-out rectangle. Replace the cake pieces in the tunnel over the fluff, covering all of it. Turn the cake over onto a serving plate so the cut-out side is on the bottom. Cover the cake loosely with plastic wrap and chill for 1 hour.

FOR THE GANACHE

Place the chocolate in a small bowl. Heat the heavy cream in a small saucepan until it is simmering and just about to boil. Pour the cream over the chocolate, cover the bowl with plastic wrap, and let sit for 5 minutes. Remove the plastic wrap and use a butter knife to stir the chocolate into the cream until it is completely smooth. Let the mixture cool to almost room temperature. Once cool and ready to use, stir the ganache a few times before using.

TO ASSEMBLE

Remove the chilled cake from the fridge and pour the ganache over the top, letting it drip down the sides, if desired. Let the ganache set until just tacky, then add the toasted marshmallows to the top. Serve cold or at room temperature. This cake can be stored covered (without the marshmallows) in the refrigerator for 24 hours.

NOTE

If you only have a tube pan with a removable bottom, you may want to wrap the bottom of the pan in foil before baking. The cake batter is thin and can leak if your pan is two pieces.

Hot Chocolate Cake

Confetti Cake

Spring is just around the corner, isn't it? Maybe for those of you on the coasts, but here in the Upper Midwest, we still have promises to keep, and miles to go before we sleep* . . . so I'll do my best to keep you going with a bright and cheery cake to make for birthdays, for just-because days, or for we-haven't-seen-the-sun-in-months days. (*Robert Frost, "Stopping by Woods on a Snowy Evening")

CAKE

1 scant cup [210 g] large egg whites (from 6 or 7 eggs), at room temperature

1 cup [240 g] whole milk, at room temperature

½ cup [120 g] Crème Fraîche (page 205) or sour cream, at room temperature

1 tablespoon pure vanilla extract

2¾ cups [391 g] all-purpose flour, plus more for coating the pans

2 cups [400 g] granulated sugar

4 teaspoons baking powder

1 teaspoon salt

1 cup [2 sticks or 227 g] unsalted butter, at room temperature, cut into 1 in [2.5 cm] pieces, plus more for greasing the pans

¾ cup [115 g] sprinkles (see notes, page 184)

CREAM CHEESE ICING

1 cup [2 sticks or 227 g] unsalted butter, at room temperature

8 oz [226 g] cream cheese, at room temperature

2 tablespoons light corn syrup

Pinch salt

4½ cups [540 g] confectioners' sugar

1 tablespoon pure vanilla extract

FOR THE CAKE

Adjust an oven rack to the middle position and preheat the oven to 350°F [180°C]. Butter and flour two 8 by 2 in [20 by 5 cm] round cake pans (see notes, page 184) and line the bottoms with parchment paper (see page 16).

continued

183

In a medium bowl or liquid measuring cup, whisk together the egg whites, milk, crème fraîche, and vanilla. • In the bowl of a stand mixer fitted with a paddle, combine the flour, granulated sugar, baking powder, and salt. • With the mixer running on low speed, add the butter one piece at a time, beating until the mixture resembles coarse sand. With the mixer still running on low speed, slowly add a little more than half the wet ingredients. Increase the speed to medium and beat until the ingredients are incorporated, about 30 seconds. With the mixer running on low speed, add the rest of the wet ingredients, mixing until just combined. Increase the speed to medium and beat for 20 seconds (the batter may still look a little bumpy). Scrape down the sides and bottom of the bowl, add the sprinkles, and use a spatula to mix the batter a few more times, incorporating the sprinkles and making sure everything is completely combined. • Divide the batter between the prepared pans and smooth the tops. Tap the pans gently on the counter twice each to help get rid of any air bubbles. Bake for 30 to 38 minutes, rotating the pans halfway through, until the cakes are golden brown and a wooden skewer or toothpick inserted into the center comes out with a faint bit of crumbs, or a finger gently pressed into the top leaves a slight indentation. • Transfer the pans to a wire rack and let cool for 30 minutes. Turn the cakes out onto the rack, remove the parchment paper, and let cool completely. Once cool, the cakes can be frosted or wrapped in plastic and refrigerated overnight. Unfrosted cakes can also be wrapped in plastic and frozen for up to 1 week.

FOR THE ICING

In the bowl of a stand mixer fitted with a paddle, beat the butter and cream cheese on medium speed until light yellow and creamy, about 3 minutes. Add the corn syrup and salt and mix on medium speed until combined. Lower the speed to low and gradually add the confectioners' sugar, then increase the speed to medium and beat until smooth and creamy, stopping to scrape down the sides of the bowl as necessary, 2 to 3 minutes. Add the vanilla and mix again on low speed until combined.

TO ASSEMBLE

Place one cake layer on a turntable or serving plate. With an offset spatula, spread the top with 1 cup [320 g] of the icing. Place the second layer on top and frost and evenly coat the cake with the remaining icing. The cake can be covered and stored in the refrigerator for 24 hours. Bring the cake to room temperature before serving.

NOTES

Large sprinkles work best in the batter— smaller sprinkles tend to melt and bleed too much. Large sprinkles will still melt, but streak beautifully rather than turn the batter a grayish color. • This cake can also be made in a 9 by 13 in [23 by 33 cm] pan, and you can also omit the sprinkles; it will be a fabulous white cake.

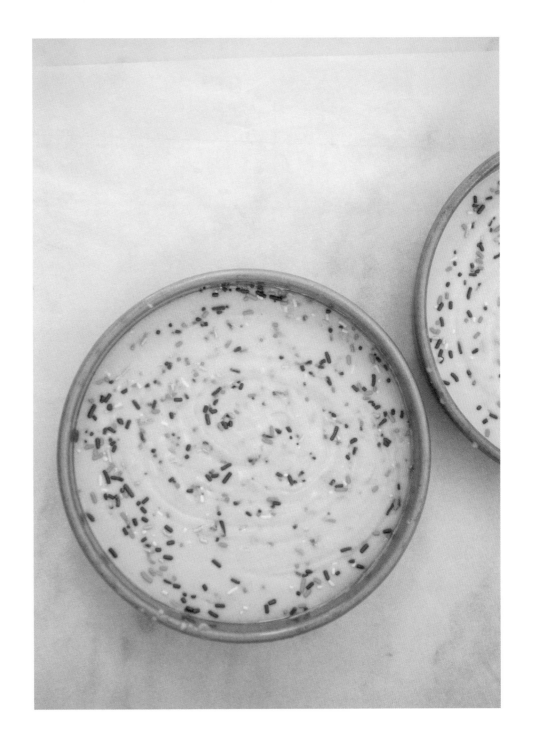

Rough Puff Pastry

This is my shortcut to puff pastry; it's not as obsessive and exacting as the real thing but still results in rich, flaky layers, just like the more labor-intensive version.

1½ cups [3 sticks or 339 g] unsalted butter, cut into 20 pieces	1 cup [240 g] ice water ½ teaspoon fresh lemon juice	2 cups [284 g] all-purpose flour, plus more for dusting	1 tablespoon granulated sugar ½ teaspoon salt

Place the butter pieces in a small bowl and transfer it to the freezer for 5 to 10 minutes. • In a liquid measuring cup, combine ¼ cup [60 g] of the ice water and the lemon juice. • In the bowl of a stand mixer fitted with a paddle, mix together the flour, sugar, and salt on low speed. Add the butter and mix on low speed until slightly incorporated. The butter will be smashed and in all different sizes, most about half their original size. • Add the lemon juice mixture and mix on low speed until the dough just holds together and looks shaggy. If the dough is still really dry and not coming together, add more ice water, 1 tablespoon at a time, until it just starts to hold. • Transfer the dough to a lightly floured work surface and flatten it slightly into a square. Gather any loose/dry pieces that won't stick to the dough

and place them on top of the square. Gently fold the dough over onto itself and then flatten into a square again. Repeat this process five or six times until all the loose pieces are worked into the dough, being careful not to overwork the dough. Flatten the dough one last time and form it into a 6 in [15 cm] square. Transfer the dough to a floured sheet pan or plate and sprinkle the top of the dough with flour. Place the dough in the refrigerator and chill until firm, 20 minutes. • Return the dough to the lightly floured work surface and roll it into an 8 by 16 in [20 by 40.5 cm] rectangle. If the dough sticks at all, sprinkle more flour underneath it. Brush any excess flour off the dough and, using a bench scraper, fold the short ends of the dough over the middle to make three layers, similar to a business letter. This is the first turn.

(If the dough still looks shaggy, don't worry, it will become smooth and even out as you keep rolling.) • Flip the dough over (seam-side down), give the dough a quarter turn, and roll away from you, this time into a 6 by 16 in [15 by 40.5 cm] rectangle. Fold the short ends over the middle. This is the second turn. • Sprinkle the top of the dough with flour and return it to the sheet pan and refrigerate for 20 minutes. Return the dough to the work surface and repeat the process of folding the dough, creating the third and fourth turns. After the last turn, gently use a rolling pin to compress the layers together slightly. Wrap the dough tightly in plastic wrap and chill for at least 1 hour before using, or keep refrigerated for up to 2 days.

5

"Now, too, I perceive my first experience of the dreary sensation—often to return in after-life—of being unable, next day, to get back to the dull, settled world; of wanting to live for ever in the bright atmosphere I have quitted...as my eye wanders down the branches of my Christmas Tree."

—CHARLES DICKENS, *A CHRISTMAS TREE*

Extras

Caramel Shards

I came across caramel shards in Pierre Hermé's book *Macarons*; he uses them finely processed as filling in his famous cookies. I love trying to sneak crunchiness into most of my desserts, and found this to be a clever way to do so.

½ cup [100 g] granulated sugar

¼ cup [80 g] light corn syrup

2 tablespoons water

¼ teaspoon salt

2 teaspoons pure vanilla extract

Line a sheet pan with parchment paper. • In a large, heavy-bottom saucepan, combine the sugar, corn syrup, water, and salt, stirring very gently while trying to avoid getting any sugar crystals on the sides of the pan. Cover the pan and bring to a boil over medium-high heat until the sugar has melted and the mixture is clear, 3 to 5 minutes. Uncover and cook until the mixture has turned a pale golden color, 4 to 5 minutes more, and registers about 300°F [150°C] on an instant-read thermometer. Turn the heat down slightly, and cook for a few minutes more, until the sugar is golden and registers 350°F [180°C] on an instant-read thermometer. Immediately remove the pan from the heat and add the vanilla, stirring to combine. • Pour the caramel onto the prepared sheet pan and tip the sheet pan back and forth until the caramel is in a thin, even layer, about ¼ in [6 mm] thick. • Let the caramel harden, then cut it with a knife for larger pieces, or break it up and process the pieces in a food processor for very small shards. Caramel shards can be stored in an airtight container at room temperature for up to 2 weeks.

191

Extras

Marshmallows

I didn't realize how superior homemade marshmallows were until I tried them; they are heads and tails above the supermarket versions. They also toast much better, with a deep amber char.

¾ cup [90 g] confectioners' sugar

¼ cup [28 g] cornstarch

5 teaspoons gelatin

½ cup [120 g] cold water, plus ½ cup [120 g] room-temperature water

2 cups [400 g] granulated sugar

¼ cup [80 g] corn syrup

¼ teaspoon salt

2 large egg whites, at room temperature

¼ teaspoon cream of tartar

1 tablespoon pure vanilla extract

Grease a 9 by 13 in [23 by 33 cm] baking pan. • In a small bowl, whisk together the confectioners' sugar and cornstarch. • In a small bowl, combine the gelatin and cold water. • In a medium, heavy-bottom saucepan fitted with an instant-read thermometer, combine the granulated sugar, room-temperature water, corn syrup, and salt. Bring to a boil over medium-high heat until the temperature reaches 240°F [115°C], 4 to 5 minutes. Immediately remove from the heat and whisk in the gelatin. • In the bowl of a stand mixer fitted with a whisk, whip the egg whites and cream of tartar on medium-high speed until soft peaks form, 2 to 3 minutes. • With the mixer running on low speed, pour the hot syrup along the side of the bowl, being careful not to hit the whisk. Increase the speed to medium-high and whisk until the mixture has doubled in volume and is thick and glossy, and the sides of the bowl have cooled, 8 to 10 minutes. Add the vanilla and mix on low speed until combined.

continued

Scrape into the prepared pan and use an offset spatula to smooth the top of the mixture. Sift 2 to 3 tablespoons of the confectioners' sugar mixture over the top. Let sit overnight at room temperature, uncovered, until firm. • Remove from the pan and cut with a knife, scissors, or pizza wheel dusted with some of the confectioners' sugar mixture. Toss the cut marshmallows (a few at a time) into the remaining confectioners' sugar mixture to coat. Shake off any excess in a fine-mesh sieve. Store at room temperature in an airtight container for up to 1 week.

Marshmallows

Mint Marshmallows

Add 2 teaspoons pure mint extract (more or less as desired) to the mixture along with the vanilla. Add a few drops pink or green food coloring if desired.

Caramel

This is one of those staples that is fine store-bought but so much better homemade. It also tastes delicious poured over any of the No-Churn Ice Creams (page 196).

1¼ cups [250 g] granulated sugar

⅓ cup [80 g] water

2 tablespoons light corn syrup

½ teaspoon salt

½ cup [120 g] heavy cream

5 tablespoons [70 g] unsalted butter, cut into 5 pieces

1 tablespoon pure vanilla extract

In a large, heavy-bottom saucepan (the caramel will bubble up quite a bit once it starts cooking, so it's important to have a deep pan), combine the sugar, water, corn syrup, and salt, stirring very gently to combine while trying to avoid getting any sugar crystals on the sides of the pan. Cover the pan and bring to a boil over medium-high heat until the sugar has melted and the mixture is clear, 3 to 5 minutes. Uncover and cook until the mixture has turned a light golden color. Turn the heat down to medium and cook until it turns a deep golden color and registers 340°F [170°C] on an instant-read thermometer. Immediately remove the pan from the heat and add the heavy cream. The cream will foam considerably, so be careful pouring it in. Add the butter next, followed by the vanilla, and stir to combine. Set aside to cool. Caramel can be refrigerated in an airtight container for up to 2 weeks.

195

Extras

VARIATION

Salted Caramel

When you take the caramel off the heat, add ½ teaspoon fleur de sel. Stir to combine.

No-Churn Ice Cream

I include no-churn ice cream recipes in all my books; I find them a welcome alternative to churning homemade ice cream, as they take less time and don't need fancy machinery. I've included my basic recipe here, as well as a few new variations that pair well with recipes in this book.

One 14 oz [397 g] can sweetened condensed milk	1 tablespoon pure vanilla extract 1 vanilla bean, seeds scraped (optional)	¼ teaspoon salt 2 oz [57 g] cream cheese, at room temperature	2 cups [240 g] heavy cream

In a large bowl, whisk together the sweetened condensed milk, vanilla, vanilla bean seeds, if using, and salt until completely combined. • In the bowl of a stand mixer fitted with a whisk, beat the cream cheese on medium speed until smooth. Lower the speed to low and add the heavy cream in a slow, steady stream, mixing until combined. Increase the speed to medium-high and whisk until stiff peaks form, 3 to 4 minutes. • Add half of the whipped cream mixture to the sweetened condensed milk mixture and whisk until completely combined. Using a rubber spatula, gently fold in the remaining whipped cream mixture until no streaks remain. Pour the mixture into a 9 by 4 by 4 in [23 by 10 by 10 cm] Pullman loaf pan with a lid and freeze until firm, 6 hours, or for up to 1 week.

NOTE

If you don't have a Pullman pan, a regular 9 in [23 cm] loaf pan covered with plastic wrap will work too.

VARIATIONS

Chocolate No-Churn Ice Cream

Melt 8 oz [226 g] of semisweet or bittersweet chocolate. Pour 5 oz [142 g] of
the chocolate onto a sheet pan lined with parchment paper and freeze until
firm, 10 to 15 minutes. Add the remaining 3 oz [85 g] of melted chocolate to the
sweetened condensed milk mixture. Chop the cold chocolate into bite-size pieces
and add it to the finished ice cream mixture before pouring it into the loaf pan.

continued

Coffee No-Churn Ice Cream

Add ½ cup [120 g] of room-temperature brewed espresso or strong coffee and ½ teaspoon of ground espresso to the sweetened condensed milk mixture.

Pumpkin No-Churn Ice Cream

Add ¾ cup [168 g] of unsweetened pumpkin purée, ½ teaspoon of ground cinnamon, ¼ teaspoon of ground ginger, ¼ teaspoon of freshly grated nutmeg, and a pinch of cloves to the sweetened condensed milk mixture.

Salted Caramel No-Churn Ice Cream

Make the no-churn ice cream as directed in the main recipe. Pour half of the ice cream mixture into the Pullman pan, then dollop ½ cup [180 g] of Caramel (page 195), Salted Caramel variation, over the ice cream. Use the tip of a butter knife to swirl the mixture into the ice cream. Pour the remaining ice cream on top, then dollop with another ½ cup [180 g] of Caramel. Swirl again with the butter knife. Freeze as directed.

Blood Orange No-Churn Ice Cream

Add ½ cup [120 g] of blood orange juice, 1 tablespoon of triple sec, and 2 teaspoons of grated blood orange zest to the sweetened condensed milk mixture.

Candy Cane No-Churn Ice Cream

Add ½ cup [100 g] of crushed candy canes and 1 teaspoon of mint extract (or more or less to taste) to the sweetened condensed milk mixture.

Pastry Cream

Pastry cream is used in my Cruffin recipe (page 174) but also has many other applications. It can be used to replace the cream cheese filling in the Cranberries and Cream Danish (page 47). And, if you have leftover pastry cream, you can add room-temperature butter to it, whip it up in your stand mixer, and turn it into buttercream (this is known as German buttercream, or crème mousseline). Just use 1 cup (2 sticks or 227 g) of butter to 2 cups [450 g] of pastry cream.

5 egg yolks, at room temperature

1¼ cups [250 g] granulated sugar

¼ teaspoon salt

1 vanilla bean, seeds scraped, pod reserved

¼ cup [28 g] cornstarch

1 cup [240 g] whole milk

1 cup [240 g] heavy cream

1 tablespoon unsalted butter

2 teaspoons pure vanilla extract

In the bowl of a stand mixer fitted with a paddle, beat the egg yolks on low speed. With the mixer running on low speed, slowly add the sugar, followed by the salt and vanilla bean seeds, and increase the speed to medium-high (see note, page 200). Beat the egg-sugar mixture until very thick and pale yellow, about 5 minutes. Scrape down the sides of the bowl and add the cornstarch, then mix on low speed until combined. • In a medium, heavy-bottom saucepan over medium-low heat, warm the milk, heavy cream, and vanilla bean pod until just about to simmer. Remove the pan from the heat and pour the mixture into a medium liquid measuring cup with a pourable spout.

199

continued

With the mixer running on low speed, very slowly add the hot milk mixture, leaving the pod behind in the pan. Mix until completely combined. Transfer the mixture back to the saucepan and cook over medium-low heat, stirring constantly with a wooden spoon, until the pastry cream becomes very thick and begins to boil, 5 to 7 minutes. Switch to a whisk and whisk the mixture until the pastry cream thickens and is glossy and smooth, 3 to 4 minutes. Remove the pan from the heat and strain the pastry cream through a fine-mesh sieve into a medium bowl. Stir in the butter and vanilla. Cover with plastic wrap, making sure the wrap sits directly on top of the cream (this will help keep it from forming a skin). Place in the refrigerator until well chilled. Use right away or keep refrigerated in an airtight container for 4 to 5 days.

NOTE

If the egg yolks are left alone with sugar, the sugar can burn the yolk, causing it to harden and form little egg yolk bits in whatever you are making. Make sure to continuously whisk the yolks while adding sugar.

Candied Citrus Peels

Any attempts to make candied citrus peels in my past were foiled by one key direction I missed: boiling and re-boiling the peels several times in fresh water to help eliminate their bitter edge. Once I learned this important step, I was able to make delicious candied fruit worth the time and effort.

| 4 oranges or lemons, scrubbed | 3½ cups [700 g] granulated sugar, plus more for coating | 3 cups [720 g] water | 3 tablespoons light corn syrup |

After washing the fruit really well, carefully cut off the peels in large pieces. Use a sharp paring knife to cut off and discard any excess pith, then cut the peels into ¼ to ½ in [6 to 12 mm] strips. • Fill a large pot with water and bring to a boil over medium-high heat. Add the strips to the pot and boil for 5 minutes, then strain and rinse the strips. Refill the pot with fresh water and repeat this process of boiling and straining three more times. • After the final boil, move the strips to a plate. Add the sugar, water, and corn syrup to the pot and cook over medium heat until the sugar has dissolved. Add the blanched strips of peel and cook over medium-low heat until the strips are translucent, 1½ to 2 hours. • Set a wire rack over a sheet pan lined with parchment paper. Transfer the citrus peels to the wire rack and let them sit at room temperature for 8 hours or overnight to dry. Toss the peels in sugar to coat, then store in an airtight container at room temperature for up to 3 weeks.

201

Extras

Cranberry Jam

I use this simple jam throughout the book. It also tastes delicious with Thanksgiving dinner.

½ cup [100 g] granulated sugar

¼ teaspoon salt

½ teaspoon ground cinnamon (optional)

¼ cup [60 g] water

6 oz [170 g] fresh cranberries

In a medium nonreactive saucepan over medium heat, bring the sugar, salt, cinnamon, if using, and water to a boil, stirring occasionally, until the sugar has dissolved. Stir in the cranberries and let simmer until the cranberries have popped and the jam has thickened, 15 to 20 minutes. Let cool to room temperature before using. The jam can be refrigerated in an airtight container for up to 5 days.

Streusel

I often keep a bag of streusel in my freezer and find it comes in quite handy. I use it on top of the Streusel Coffee Cake (page 63), but also often throw it on top of banana bread, muffins, Bundt cakes, and the like.

1⅓ cups [189 g] all-purpose flour

1 cup [100 g] almond flour

⅔ cup [135 g] granulated sugar

⅔ cup [135 g] light brown sugar

1 tablespoon ground cinnamon

¼ teaspoon salt

12 tablespoons [1½ sticks or 170 g] unsalted butter, at room temperature, cut into 12 pieces

In the bowl of a stand mixer fitted with a paddle, combine the all-purpose and almond flours, granulated and brown sugars, cinnamon, and salt on low speed. Add the butter one piece at a time, until the mixture comes together but is still quite crumbly. Store the streusel in an airtight container in the refrigerator for up to 1 week, or freeze in a freezer-safe bag for up to 1 month.

Whipped Cream

Homemade whipped cream is so delicious and really simple to make.

1½ cups [360 g] heavy cream	2 tablespoons granulated sugar	2 teaspoons pure vanilla extract	Pinch salt

Ten minutes before whipping the cream, place the bowl and whisk from a stand mixer in the freezer and let chill. In a stand mixer fitted with the chilled whisk, whisk together the heavy cream, sugar, vanilla, and salt in the chilled bowl on low speed for 30 to 45 seconds. Increase the speed to medium and beat for 30 to 45 seconds. Increase the speed to high and beat until the cream is smooth, thick, and nearly double in volume, 30 to 60 seconds. The whipped cream can be made 2 hours ahead of time and stored in an airtight container in the refrigerator.

Crème Fraîche

Crème fraîche is similar to sour cream but is less sour and often has a higher percentage of butterfat. It also withstands heat much better than sour cream and doesn't break when introduced to high temperatures.

3 cups [720 g]
heavy cream

¾ cup [180 g]
buttermilk

In a large bowl, whisk together the cream and buttermilk. Cover the top of the bowl with several layers of cheesecloth and place a rubber band or tie a string around the bowl to keep the cheesecloth in place. Let the bowl sit out at room temperature for 24 hours and up to 3 days until it has thickened considerably. (The time it needs to sit depends on the temperature inside your home; cold winter days will cause the mixture to take much longer to thicken than hot summer ones.) When it is thick and ready to use, gently stir the mixture and transfer it to an airtight container. Refrigerate the mixture for up to 1 week.

NOTE
Buttermilk contains active cultures ("good" bacteria) that prevent the cream from spoiling and is acidic enough to deter "bad" bacteria from growing.

205

Candied Nuts

Nuts are perfect by their lonesome, but adding some caramelized sugar and salt makes them extraordinary. They make a great addition to cakes and confections.

½ cup [100 g] granulated sugar

2 tablespoons water

¼ teaspoon salt

2 cups [280 g] walnuts, peanuts, hazelnuts, cashews, or almonds

Line a sheet pan with parchment paper. In a large skillet over medium heat, stir together the sugar, water, and salt. Cook until the sugar begins to melt, then add the nuts, stirring almost constantly until the nuts are toasted and lightly caramelized. Pour the nuts onto the prepared sheet pan and let them cool completely before chopping. Nuts can be stored in an airtight container for up to 1 week.

207

Lemon Curd

I've never been crazy about store-bought lemon curd and find that making it is worth all the effort involved. I leave out the zest for a smooth, not-too-tart curd, but you can add some to ramp up the lemon flavor if desired (see note).

8 tablespoons [1 stick or 113 g] unsalted butter, at room temperature

1½ cups [250 g] granulated sugar

¼ teaspoon salt

5 large egg yolks plus 1 large egg, at room temperature

⅓ cup [80 g] fresh lemon juice

In the bowl of a stand mixer fitted with a paddle, beat the butter on medium speed until creamy, about 1 minute. Add the sugar and salt and mix on medium speed until combined, 1 minute more. Scrape down the sides of the mixing bowl and add the egg yolks on low speed. Increase the speed to medium and beat until smooth and light, 3 to 4 minutes. Add the whole egg and mix on low speed until combined, then add the lemon juice and mix on low speed until combined, scraping down the sides as needed. • Transfer the mixture to a medium, heavy-bottom saucepan. Cook over medium heat, stirring constantly with a spatula, until the curd becomes very thick, about 10 minutes, or registers 170°F [75°C] on an instant-read thermometer; the mixture should coat a spatula at this point. Strain the mixture through a fine-mesh sieve into a medium bowl, then cover with plastic wrap, making sure the wrap sits directly on top of the curd (this will help keep it from forming a skin). Place in the refrigerator until well chilled. The curd can be stored in the refrigerator in an airtight container for up to 5 days.

NOTE

Add 2 tablespoons of lemon zest to the mixing bowl with the granulated sugar for a lemon curd with a tarter, more acidic flavor.

Blood Orange Curd

Replace the lemon juice with ½ cup [120 g] of blood orange juice.

Passion Fruit Curd

Replace the lemon juice with ½ cup [120 g] of passion fruit purée.

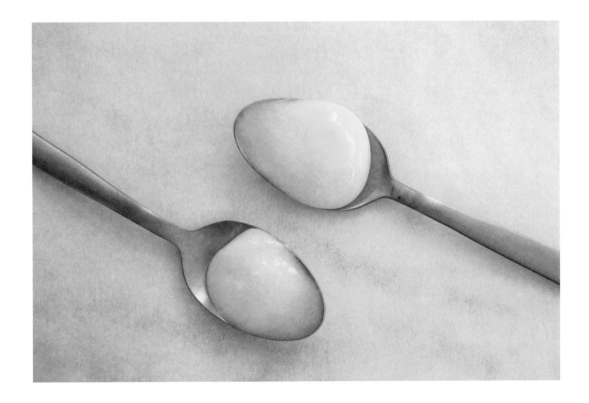

Marshmallow Fluff

Marshmallow fluff is the softer side of marshmallows, and I use it in my Hot Chocolate Cake (page 178). It is also delicious sandwiched in cookies, and would pair nicely with the Red Velvet Crinkle Cookies (page 127).

4 large egg whites

½ teaspoon cream of tartar

2 tablespoons cold water, plus ½ cup [120 g] room-temperature water

1 teaspoon gelatin

1 cup [320 g] corn syrup

1 cup [200 g] granulated sugar

¼ teaspoon salt

1 tablespoon pure vanilla extract

In the bowl of a stand mixer fitted with a whisk, whip the egg whites and cream of tartar on medium-high speed until soft peaks form, 2 to 3 minutes. • In a small bowl, combine the cold water and the gelatin. • In a medium, heavy-bottom saucepan fitted with an instant-read thermometer, combine the corn syrup, sugar, room-temperature water, and salt. Bring to a boil over medium-high heat until the temperature reaches 240°F [115°C]; this will take a few minutes. Immediately remove the saucepan from the heat and whisk in the gelatin mixture. With the stand mixer running on low speed, carefully pour the hot sugar syrup along the side of the mixing bowl, being careful not to hit the whisk attachment as you pour. When all the syrup is in the bowl, turn up the speed to medium-high and continue whisking until the mixture has doubled in volume and is quite thick and glossy, and the sides of the bowl have cooled, 8 to 10 minutes. Add the vanilla and mix until combined. Transfer the mixture to an airtight container and store in the refrigerator for up to 1 week.

Closing Out the Year

I spent eleven holiday seasons in a row working various retail jobs, everything from cashier to bookseller to barista. The stores started pumping out holiday cheer the second Thanksgiving ended, with customers piling into seemingly mile-long lines that continued up until Christmas Eve at exactly 4 p.m. when the store gates finally clanged shut and stayed that way for one whole day. Work shifts in December were spent answering the constantly ringing phone, running around the store trying to find would-be presents, making drink after espresso drink for frazzled consumers, standing at the cash register swiping credit cards for hours, and dreading the thirty-minute playlist turnovers when Paul McCartney's "Wonderful Christmastime" would come on again. And then at last, the night before Christmas, the store gate would finally shut (although people were often begging outside it: *Please, can I buy just one pound of coffee? I just need one more book for my sister-in-law, will you let me in?*). All the employees would rush around, frantically cleaning up various messes: wiping coffee spills from tables, gathering giant piles of books from every possible corner of the store and returning them to their shelves, and peeling magazines off the bathroom floor. An assistant manager would order a pizza, and we'd munch in silence before taking off to our various celebrations, sniffly and glassy-eyed, ambivalent to any sugarplums that might be dancing nearby as we wished only to crash headlong into a bed.

I've now had twelve years off from working retail shifts over the holiday season; my current job allows for more time at home during Christmas than I had in the bustling stores. I always spend the time at home, quietly listening to holiday music while baking a batch of cookies, snuggling with my little ones reading books together, or watching holiday movie marathons before heading to my parents' house early for festivities. I have a no-shopping rule on Christmas Eve for myself, but I must admit I feel something lacking each year. The month of

December doesn't feel as complete to me without all the noise and the crowds of people, Mariah Carey letting us all know what she wants through the loud-speakers from open to close, and racing up and down stairs trying to find books for exasperated customers. The thing I didn't want to make the holiday about has now ended up defining it for me. Those formative years of my teens and twenties, working so hard for hours on end, now shape how I need Christmas to *feel* to me as an adult. I can't escape that, somehow.

As in all things, I must constantly remind myself that although something feels a certain way, that doesn't mean that's how it actually is. I've been conditioned to associate some kind of hustle and bustle with the holiday season, but it's really the time spent together with my family—slowing down, savoring small moments—where I've found actual joy.

As an adult member of my family unit, I now hold quite a bit of sway in how the season will look for those I share it with; I set traditions and design them for both enjoyment and recognition. Through each tradition, I see my kids feeling so many things and getting swept up in this time—the shopping, the presents, the decorations, and the get-togethers. But I want to convey to my people that the holidays are more than that; I want them to know what the reason behind this month-long, money-spending, jingle-belling really is. At the very core, it's to look to others, to give with no expectation of getting anything in return, and to remember that we all belong to each other, all of us, across this ever-spinning snow globe that's so easily shaken.

No matter how the actual days of December end up shaping my family, I want them to be able reach past how they feel and instead know, deep down, the joy and hope of Christmas and their capacity to bring it everywhere they go.

"Ring out, wild bells,
to the wild sky,
The flying cloud,
the frosty light;
The year is dying in the night;
Ring out, wild bells,
and let him die.
Ring out the old,
ring in the new,
Ring happy bells,
across the snow;
The year is going, let him go;
Ring out the false,
ring in the true."

—FROM "RING OUT, WILD BELLS"
BY ALFRED, LORD TENNYSON

OSCAR PETERSON *An Oscar Peterson Christmas*

MARIAH CAREY *Merry Christmas*

AMY GRANT *A Christmas Album*

ELLA FITZGERALD *Ella Wishes You a Swinging Christmas*

VARIOUS ARTISTS *Ultra-Lounge: Christmas Cocktails, Part One*

BING CROSBY *A Merry Christmas with Bing Crosby & The Andrews Sisters*

DUKE PEARSON *Merry Ole Soul*

THE COUNT BASIE ORCHESTRA *A Very Swingin' Basie Christmas!*

INGRID MICHAELSON *Ingrid Michaelson's Songs for the Season*

LEIF SHIRES *Cool Jazz Christmas*

DAVID IAN *The Vintage Christmas Collection*

OVER THE RHINE *Snow Angels*

VINCE GUARALDI TRIO *A Charlie Brown Christmas*

BLONDFIRE *Holiday EP*

VARIOUS ARTISTS *The Classic Big Band Christmas Album*

MUSIC TO BAKE TO

Baking for the Holidays Playlist on Apple Music:
https://apple.co/3a1oV0e

Baking for the Holidays Playlist on Spotify:
https://spoti.fi/3sczEfK

CONVERSIONS

Commonly Used Ingredients

1 cup flour = 142 g	1 cup cocoa powder = 100 g	1 cup heavy cream = 240 g
1 cup granulated sugar = 200 g	1 cup butter (2 sticks) = 227 g	1 cup sour cream = 240 g
1 cup brown sugar = 200 g	1 egg white = 35 g	1 cup cream cheese (8 oz) = 226 g
1 cup confectioners' sugar = 120 g	1 cup whole milk = 240 g	

Oven Temperatures

300°F = 150°C	375°F = 190°C	425°F = 220°C
350°F = 180°C	400°F = 200°C	450°F = 230°C

Weights

½ oz = 14 g	3 oz = 85 g	8 oz = 226 g
1 oz = 28 g	3½ oz = 99 g	10 oz = 283 g
1½ oz = 45 g	4 oz = 113 g	12 oz = 340 g
2 oz = 57 g	4½ oz = 128 g	16 oz = 455 g
2½ oz = 71 g	5 oz = 142 g	

BIBLIOGRAPHY

Much of my baking training was hands-on experience that took place in the workplace, and many ideas, techniques, and recipe evolutions were picked up here and there over the years. It would be impossible to cite everything and everyone, but I must acknowledge (with so much gratitude) Larry and Colleen Wolner and Zoë François for their mentorship, guidance, and encouragement (you can sample the Wolners' amazing baked goods at The Blue Heron Coffeehouse in Winona, Minnesota. And Zoë offers help to all on her beautiful website, zoebakes.com, and her Instagram, @zoebakes).

Over the years, many books have both taught me new techniques and guided my baking knowledge. Here are some that have inspired a starting point or answered a baking question for this book.

Ansel, Dominique. *Dominique Ansel: The Secret Recipes*. New York: Simon & Schuster, 2014.

Arefi, Yossy. *Sweeter off the Vine*. Berkeley: Ten Speed Press, 2016.

Editors at America's Test Kitchen. *The Perfect Cookie*. Brookline, MA: America's Test Kitchen, 2017.

François, Zoë. *Zoë Bakes Cakes*. Berkeley: Ten Speed Press, 2021.

Hermé, Pierre. *Macaron*. New York: Abrams, 2015.

Keller, Thomas. *Bouchon Bakery*. New York: Artisan, 2012.

Lee, Mandy. *The Art of Escapism Cooking*. New York: Harper Collins Publishers, 2019.

Lin, Irvin. *Marbled, Swirled, and Layered*. Boston: Houghton Mifflin Harcourt, 2016.

O'Brady, Tara. *Seven Spoons*. Berkeley: Ten Speed Press, 2015.

Ojakangas, Beatrice. *The Great Holiday Baking Book*. Minneapolis: University of Minnesota Press, 2001.

Ottolenghi, Yotam, and Helen Goh. *Sweet*. New York: Ten Speed Press, 2017.

Page, Karen, and Andrew Dorenburg. *The Flavor Bible*. New York: Little, Brown and Company, 2008.

Prueitt, Elisabeth, and Chad Robertson. *Tartine: A Classic Revisited*. San Francisco: Chronicle Books, 2019.

Reed, Jessica. *The Baker's Appendix*. New York: Clarkson Potter, 2017.

Sever, Shauna. *Midwest Made*. New York: Running Press, 2019.

Sönmezsoy, Cenk. *The Artful Baker*. New York: Abrams, 2017.

Wood, Phoebe, and Kirsten Jenkins. *The Pie Project*. Australia: Hardie Grant Books, 2016.

RESOURCES

Breville
Kitchen equipment and essentials | *breville.com*

Emile Henry
Ceramic cookware | *emilehenryusa.com*

Guittard Chocolate Company
Chocolates and cocoa powder | *guittard.com*

King Arthur Flour
Specialty flours and baking items | *kingarthurflour.com*

Land O'Lakes
Unsalted and European butter | *landolakes.com*

Material
Beautiful and functional kitchen knives | *materialkitchen.com*

Mauviel
Copper cookware | *mauviel.com*

Nordic Ware
Baking pans and kitchen necessities | *nordicware.com*

Valrhona
Chocolates and cocoa powder | *valrhona-chocolate.com*

Williams Sonoma
Bakeware, baking utensils, and decorating tools | *williams-sonoma.com*

You can also find my favorite kitchen items at my
Amazon storefront | *amazon.com/shop/sarah_kieffer*

ACKNOWLEDGMENTS

First and foremost, thank you to all the *Vanilla Bean Blog* readers! This book wouldn't be here without all of you, and I appreciate your support.

Thank you to Chronicle Books, and my editors Sarah Billingsley, Cristina Garces, and Deanne Katz. I have truly enjoyed the book-writing process with you, and it means so much as an author to know that my book is in good hands and that you truly care about making a book *together*. Thank you to Lizzie Vaughan for yet again another amazing book design; your attention to detail and thoughtfulness shine. Thank you to Cynthia Shannon and Joyce Lin for your excellent advice, patience, and expertise—you are both truly amazing. And to Margo Winton Parodi—I am always humbled by and grateful for your copyediting expertise.

To Jane Dystel, my literary agent, thank you for your guidance and help. Your ideas and counsel are always wise, and I am thankful to be in such good hands.

To Scott Beck, thank you for constantly taking care of us. I am thankful for your friendship.

To my recipe testers: THANK YOU. You have been along for several books now, and your time and (very honest) feedback are appreciated: Kelsey Tenney, Molly Hayes, Lindsay Reine, Colleen Wolner, Anna Wolner, Heidi Smith, Joel Peck, Heather Meyen, and Mark Neufang.

Always, so many thank-yous to Zoë François for being such a great friend, and for always lending your support.

To all the grandmas and grandpas: Thank you for babysitting when needed, always being encouraging, and for all the the taste testing. I appreciate you all so much.

To Winter and River: Thank you for your patience and encouragement. I am grateful for you each and every day.

To my Adam A: Thank you for washing dishes, cleaning up after me, and always cheering for me. You'll always be my favorite one.

INDEX

Photo by Adam Kieffer

SARAH KIEFFER spent many years baking at coffeehouses and bakeries in Minneapolis and the surrounding area before starting her website, *The Vanilla Bean Blog* (which won *Saveur*'s Best Baking & Dessert Blog award in 2014). Her pan-banging cookie technique went viral after she introduced it in the *New York Times*. Sarah is the author of *100 Cookies*, and her work has been featured on *Good Morning America*, as well as in *Food & Wine*, *Food52*, *Cherry Bombe*, *The Kitchn*, and more. When she is not baking, you can find her reading and rereading favorite books, spending time with her family, and drinking too much coffee.

CHRONICLE BOOKS publishes distinctive books and gifts. From award-winning children's titles, bestselling cookbooks, and eclectic pop culture to acclaimed works of art and design, stationery, and journals, we craft publishing that's instantly recognizable for its spirit and creativity. Enjoy our publishing and become part of our community at www.chroniclebooks.com.